D1557035

LONESOME ROAD

GEORGE HARSH

LONESOME
ROAD

W · W · NORTON & COMPANY · INC ·

NEW YORK

Library of Congress Catalog Card No. 69-14699

SNB 393 07456 0

2 3 4 5 6 7 8 9 0

"Oh, the horror of it!" cried the King, "I shall never, never forget it!"

"You will though," said the Queen, "unless you make a memorandum of it."

— *Through the Looking Glass*

INTRODUCTION

Somehow it seems to me an act of monumental self-esteem for anyone to write an autobiography. It would appear to be a manifestation of what a
friend of mine calls The Peacock Syndrome. Surely, if
"auto" was worth writing about, if he had some new point
of view worth considering, and if his biographer had some
writing talent, his biography might be worth reading.

But autobiographies bring questions to my mind. To
begin with, there is the question of vindication. The subject
of an autobiography is judged by his intentions, while the
subject of a biography is judged by his deeds. There is a
sea of difference. In writing this, I have tried to keep this
difference in mind. I hope the reader will do the same.

Then there is always the question of honesty—self-
honesty. No matter how scrupulously honest the writer may
try to be, an autobiography is at best a series of connected
memories, impressions, and recollections of himself—and

the events of his life—all thrown into the hopper and then screened through the judgment of the writer. And how many autobiographies ever ruthlessly hold up for inspection the mean, petty, despicable qualities that are in all us saints and sinners and make us what we really are? All autobiographies should be entitled *It Seems to Me*.

It would be presumptuous of me to make the statement that "All life is a mass of paradoxes, contradictions, and ironies"; I just don't know about "all life." I only know that my life has been a mass of paradoxes, contradictions, and ironies. And when the reader finishes these pages I feel he will agree.

Life started out for me with great expectations. I lost my father when I was twelve, but at his death a half-million dollars was put in trust in my name. Then at the age of seventeen something went sour within me and I was sentenced to die in the electric chair. But there is a saying in this country: "You can't hang a million dollars." This is a colloquialism for the hard truth that there is one law for the rich and another for the poor, and at the age of eighteen my sentence was commuted to life in prison. I spent the next twelve years on a Georgia chain gang.

The ironies and the paradoxes and the contradictions kept tripping over one another. To be pardoned (because I saved a man's life) after twelve years on a chain gang and then to find myself, six months later, a commissioned pilot officer, and gentleman, in His Majesty's Royal Air Force is, I hold, something of a contradiction. And then, after two years of blasting the sleeping cities of Germany with phosphorous fire bombs and high explosives, to be shot down to spend three years in Stalag Luft III as a prisoner of war is, to my way of thinking, at least somewhat ironical.

On the face of things it would appear that these are sufficient ironies to last anyone through a long lifetime, but it is now 1970 and the ironies have never let up. I hope they never will, for life without its incongruities would be a dull puddle of mud.

Of late we have had a spate of books written by wife-killers, baby-rapers, and what not who have been saved from their fate by Barnum-like lawyers who can turn a courtroom into a three-ring circus. Almost without exception these books are protestations of the simon-pure innocence of the writer, or tirades against the inequities and stupidities of our legal system; and the tiresome phrase, "miscarriage of justice," runs through all of them like a fugue.

I would like to assure the reader that in the following pages he will not have his intelligence insulted or his mind bored by such justifications. It has been my observation that when most people cry out for justice what they actually have in mind is mercy. It's a matter of semantics, I guess. Anyway, I was duly indicted, tried, and convicted for a crime, and I was guilty as hell. I hope this does not have a ring of bravado or defiance about it, for I do not make this statement with that attitude at all. Had I received justice I would have been hanged as high as Haman, and with a length of rusty barbed wire. But instead I received mercy. A jury of twelve men sentenced me to die. This, I am convinced, was something not one of them could have done on his own. And then it took a man of rare courage, unquestioned integrity, and honesty, acting on his own and reaching within his own soul to find the needed understanding and compassion, to grant me mercy. It was a humbling, and educating, experience for me to receive mercy from a fellow human being, and I learned that men who can be cruel and cowardly can also find within themselves the qualities of mercy and bravery.

For what I did there was no excuse. Five immature college students, not stopping to weigh the potential consequences, embarked almost lightheartedly on a series of senseless crimes. As honestly as I can recall, I think committing the act in itself represented a challenge to us. The denouement would have made the gunfight at the OK Corral look like a quilting bee. When the smoke cleared two men lay dead and I was nearer death than life. To this day I have a hard time explaining it satisfactorily, even to myself.

LONESOME ROAD

I.

I was only twenty, but I had already been on the Georgia chain gang two years when he arrived. He was one of the most improbable sights I had ever seen. He was about five feet ten inches tall, and while he may have been wiry, in the poorly fitting striped clothing he looked just plain skinny and frail. He had red hair and the light, freckled complexion of the typical redhead, and I groaned inwardly as I thought of what the searing rays of the Georgia sun would do to his skin. It was hard to tell, but I judged him to be in his early or middle forties. I took all this in at a glance and made my surmises almost unconsciously, but what riveted my attention was the hat the man was wearing. In those days all new workers on the chain gang were issued wide-brimmed, floppy palmetto straw hats —hats with a sense of shelter about them—but for some reason the transfer guards had allowed him to keep his civilian hat. It was an immaculate, stiff pearl-gray Homburg, and it would have looked quite at home in the corridors of the State Department in Washington or on the banks of Quai d'Orsay in Paris, but it was the most unlikely head-gear I could think of in which to arrive at a chain gang in mid-August in south Georgia. "A nut, obviously," I thought to myself. Besides being incongruous, such a hat could only attract the unfavorable attention of the "walking boss," or foreman, Boss Bray, and the two shotgun guards, Boss Brewer and Boss Charlie; anything even slightly outside the bounds of normality was, in their ignorant minds, automatically suspicious. The delivery of new men to the work site of a chain gang would normally pique the curiosity of the whole gang, and work would momentarily slacken while the gang tried to size up the new arrivals. This slackening would be quickly noticed by Boss Bray, who, screaming like a stricken vulture in his strange, high-pitched voice, would make certain the pace was resumed before he went down and collected the commitment papers from the transfer guards.

We thirty convicts were not the only ones puzzled by this apparition climbing down from the back seat of the old, battered Model T touring car; Boss Bray was standing open-mouthed, gawking at the new arrival. The two transfer men, paying scant attention to the two new men they had brought with them, were puzzling over the sheaf of commitment papers. There was some speculation among us convicts as to whether or not these two could even read their own names.

The boy who accompanied the redhead was of a type only too prevalent on the chain gangs. He was young, perhaps seventeen, and good-looking in a pretty sort of way; and from the manner in which he handled himself I knew instinctively that he was a finished product of the reform schools. He was utterly sure of himself in this environment, unlike the redhead, who was in a state of semishock. The Kid—that was the name he was subsequently known by—had got hold of some bits of string and had tied the shackles up as high as they would go on the calves of his legs, thereby giving himself as much stride as possible while also keeping the stride chain from dragging and tripping him with every step. The new striped clothing even seemed to fit him—or he to fit it. What gave away his background though was his apparent acceptance of being where he was. He was gazing about him with mild interest and contempt and seemed quite unconcerned that at ten o'clock on a sweltering August morning he should find himself dumped onto a Georgia chain gang. I knew the type only too well.

There were two hundred and forty convicts in that camp, divided up into work gangs of twenty-five to thirty men, and of these two hundred and forty some ten of them were open and admitted "wolves"—men who had served too long either on chain gangs, behind the walls of various penitentiaries, in the coal mines of Brushy Mountain, Tennessee, or in the sugar cane brakes of Louisiana. They had some time ago given up the idea, or the hope, that they would ever again lead normal lives. It had been years since any of them had known female companionship, and being, for the most part, healthy men with natural urges and desires, they had found emotional and physical release in a manner generally considered abnormal. Most of these men had at first turned to homosexuality as a substitute, but, as so often happens, very shortly the substitute became more meaningful than the real thing, and now today there was no turning back for them. Of late there has been much open discussion on this subject, but as far as I am concerned, I have too many other things to think about to care what two consenting adults do between them.

But looking at the Kid that morning, I knew well what would soon be taking place. Many of the older wolves were comfortably and satisfactorily "married," and theirs would be but a passing desire to sample the grass in a greener pasture. For a while there would be a covert, but nonetheless spirited, competition for the favors of the Kid. Being an old and experienced hand at this sort of coquetry and enjoying every minute of it, the Kid would pit one wolf against the other until "she" finally decided which one of her suitors could do her the most material good and settled the whole thing by making her selection. Then, and not until then, those of us in that camp who still thought any sort of woman infinitely more desirable than a young boy could settle down to a normal existence without fear of being caught up as innocent bystanders in a knife fight. And knife fights there would be until this courtship was finally settled by a pledged troth.

By now Boss Bray had recovered from his surprise. "Y'gawdanned convicts!" he screamed. "Git with it! Pick up the lick!"

Dutifully we picked up the lick—that system of working whereby we bent down and shoveled dirt onto the mule-drawn wagons in unison. Those up above loosening the dirt from the side of the hill with picks also worked with the lick, and the picks rose and fell with a steady ground-throbbing rhythm. Both guards and convicts benefited from the lick system. The guards could immediately spot a malingerer, but, more important, we convicts found some relief from the drudgery of the back-breaking toil. The timing of the lick, the rhythm, the cadence that was invariably accompanied by a work chant made the whole proceeding seem like a shoddy ballet, and this made us forget the deadening monotony of what we were doing. "Pick 'em up high–ER! Let 'em fall hard–ER!"

Each time I came up with a shovelful of dirt I shot a glance down the road we were building at the new arrivals. The transfer guards were leaving in their old Ford, and Boss Bray was shepherding the new ones up to the work site. The Kid was swinging along with an easy, hobbling stride, but the redhead was tripping over his chains and almost falling with every step. I knew it would be a long time before the poor guy mastered the art of walking with short, pigeon-toed steps, swinging the foot out and then placing the heel just in front of the toes of the other foot. It took practice but after a while a veteran could almost keep up with an un-shackled man. I knew how the redhead felt; two years previously I had stumbled along in the same way.

He had undoubtedly been in the county jail for some months while the grand jury went through the process of binding him over for trial in a state superior court. After numerous delays he had finally been tried and convicted, and if he had had a lawyer, and some money, there had been the further delay of the appeals and finally the upholding of the conviction and the resentencing. During these few months he had grown accustomed to the horrors, the filth, the squalor, the rough, smelly blankets, the cockroaches, and the sickening food of the jail. Then suddenly, in the gray pre-dawn, he had been roughly awakened, snatched out of this by-now-familiar environment, and hurled headlong into an even worse situation. In jail he had heard numerous stories of the chain gangs from his fellow inmates, but no matter what he had heard, nothing could have prepared him for the reality. The deputy sheriffs had handcuffed him, probably had leg-ironed him, and then had whisked him twenty miles out into the country to the chain gang camp. Anyone who has seen an old Paul Muni or Edward G. Robinson movie is fairly familiar with the general decor of a Georgia prison camp. (I have often had the impression those two rugged actors spent more time on a chain gang than I did.) But this particular camp was a holdover from a more primitive time; it was one of the few remaining cage camps. Originally convicts were kept at night in latticework steel cages set on wheels so that teams of mules could easily move the cages from one temporary camp site to another. However, this was no longer considered feasible, so these thirty old rusting cages, their once-gaudy paint eroded and washed away by time, had been drawn up into a circle where they sat looking like forlorn and abandoned remnants of a tawdry circus. The iron-wheeled steel cages that might have once contained lions and tigers and leopards were now the sleeping quarters for those damned souls whom society had cast out. The area around the cages—some two acres of treeless, grassless, hard-packed Georgia red clay soil—was enclosed by a high barbed-wire fence with a heavy gate at one end. In the center of the circle of cages was an unpainted, weather-grayed shack which was the kitchen and mess hall. On one side of the mess shack stood another smaller shack, the latrine, and on the other side of the kitchen stood a handled pump with a forty-foot wooden trough running off from it. This water supply for the convicts was perilously close to the latrine, but, as Mark Twain said of the Ganges, I have always doubted that any self-respecting germ would have lived in it. That water would have probably gagged a maggot, but it was icy cold, and after all you can't have everything.

Outside the wire-enclosed compound, just by the gate, stood another group of unpainted, grayed shacks, which consisted of the office, the guards' quarters and kitchen and mess hall, the blacksmith shop, and several storerooms and tool sheds. Down a slight hill from this administrative complex stood a large barn and corral for the numerous mule teams. The whole thing was a desolate landscape out of hell, and any artist interested in painting that particular place (Doré, perhaps) would have to use strong brush strokes of red. During dry periods everything was covered with a red dust from that peculiar Georgia soil, and during wet seasons the whole place was a sea of red mud. It was now the dry period, and what slight and fitful breeze there was stirred up the dust and sifted it into and onto everything in the compound. At least the breeze helped dissipate the ever-present stench of urine coming from the wooden tubs that served as night latrines in each of the iron cages.

The two new arrivals had been dumped out at the office by the sheriff's deputies and had been taken over by the deputy warden and the yard foreman. These latter two had marched them into a wooden shack with a concrete floor where they had been made to strip, put their civilian clothing into wooden boxes, and then shower under a cold-water faucet. After a yellow-laundry-soap scrubbing, which hopefully would remove any jail-bred lice, they had been tossed old rags to use as towels, and then new striped clothing had been issued to them.

Next had come the bradding-on of the shackles and chains. From the combination shower-storeroom they had been led to the blacksmith shop, where Ol' Pete, a knife-scarred villain who was winding up a twenty-year sentence for running amuck and killing three people with a butcher knife, had hammered the shackles and chains about their legs. The shackles were rings of steel about the thickness of a man's index finger which were linked together by a logging chain thirteen links long. Also fastened to this stride chain was another three-foot length of chain with a large ring in the free end—the upright chain by which the wearer could be fastened with any number of his fellow convicts to a long length of heavy squad chain. As the shackles were being bradded about his ankles, the redhead must have wondered just how he was to remove his trousers through all this tangle of shackles and chains. To a new man this seemed a puzzle without solution and was just one more assault on his dignity as a human being. Later he would have to learn the trick of removing his belt, emptying his pockets, and working one leg and the crotch of his trousers down, through and free of one shackle, then pulling the freed trouser leg back up through the shackle, and repeating the process on the other leg. Even with practice it was a time-consuming and laborious business, and few of us bothered to remove our trousers except on Saturday nights when we were issued clean clothing after the official "hot" bath.

The idea of rehabilitation had no place in the Georgia penal system of those days; punishment in the Old Testament sense was the only concept even remotely considered. If in the process the prisoner's spirit could be broken and if he could be turned into a dead-eyed automaton, so much the better. It would make the guards' job easier.

After the shackles had been riveted about their ankles, the redhead and the Kid had been led to the office where the deputy warden, pecking away with two fingers at a dust-covered typewriter, had "written him up." A carbon copy of these papers would accompany him to the work site in order that the foreman and the guards to whose gang he would be assigned would have some knowledge of their new charge. Following this formality, he and the Kid had been led into the compound, where in the prisoners' mess hall they had been given the unvarying breakfast of this chain gang: a rusty tin pan piled with lumpy grits swimming in hog-grease-"thickenin' " gravy, a slab of fried sow belly, a pone of corn bread, and a cup of black chicory coffee.

These images of what the new men had just been through flashed through my mind as I watched Boss Bray march them up to the work site. He halted them just on the other side of the line of mule-drawn, trusty-driven wagons we were loading.

"Hey, Brewer . . . Charlie!" he called to the two shotgun guards. "This here redhead one's name is Heep . . . he's got eighteen to twenty years. That's a heap a' time, ain't it? Tee-hee-hee!"

That titter was one of the most unwholesome sounds I have ever heard, and if just once I had heard Bray throw back his head and give forth with a good, Falstaffian belly laugh, I might have thought there was some hope for the man.

"An' hey, Brewer," he continued with his badgering, "ya oughta hear him talk . . . la, dee, dah! He's a damn' Yankee." Then turning back to the object of his derision, he screamed, "Say sumpin', boy! Tell Boss Brewer an' Boss Charlie where ya from."

The poor man just stood there as though his feet were rooted in concrete, with an uncomprehending, blank look on his face.

"Gaw dan it!" Bray shouted. "When I say, 'Say sumpin',' I mean fer ya ta talk!" Then snatching the blackjack from his hip pocket, he knocked the gray Homburg off the man's head with a sweeping backhand swing. "Gaw dan it, talk!"

Without bothering to retrieve his hat, the man looked up toward Boss Brewer and Boss Charlie and with a stricken look on his face said quietly, "I'm from New York."

To Southern ears the *r* in *New York* seemed unduly stressed, and this simple declaration from the man brought forth more tittering from Bray and a gale of laughter from the two shotgun men. Bending down and picking up the hat, Bray crammed it crosswise over the man's head. "Aw, right, ya gawdanned Yankee . . . git over thar to that tail-end wagon an' le's see how ya shovel!" Turning around, he hollered to the trusty water boy, Grady Holloway, who was standing up on the bank watching all this, "Git some shovels down here to these new men, Grady." Whirling on the other new arrival, he shouted, "An' you, pretty boy . . . git up thar to the front wagon. Ya look like ya might be sumpin' of a smart aleck . . . wal, jist don' gimme none o' your shit . . . or I'll mess up that pretty face o' yourn!"

Four mule-drawn, trusty-driven wagons would pull into the cut, and four men were assigned to load each wagon. I was the first man loading on the last wagon, and every time I straightened up with a shovelful of dirt, my back would rub against the rump of the nigh mule. It was a mutually satisfactory arrangement, for in this manner I would rub the streaming sweat from my bare back and the mule would get his rump rubbed. These huge, long-suffering brutes were old friends of mine anyway; they too were serving life sentences, and they seemed to sense that in me they had found a kindred soul. Every morning I would fill one of my pockets with lumps of sugar from my private stock, and if I misgauged and one of them did not get his lump of sugar that morning, he would be quite cross and put out with me for the rest of the day. Survival on a chain gang required the mastering of many little seemingly inconsequential tricks. Often when the mules were between me and the guards or Boss Bray I could bend down behind the screen they afforded and miss a lick or two while I restored my aching muscles. Or during the rare instances when we were not actually working I could sag against them and in this way take some of the weight off my feet for a couple of moments. Little tricks, to be sure, but they all added up to survival. Also it was a matter of some amusement to most of us that the mules received more solicitous care than did we human convicts. Often, on extremely hot days, the mules would be pulled out to rest for a half-hour or so under the shade of the trees while we were forced to continue working.

"Gawd damn . . . ain't that sumpin'!" I remember hearing a short-termer growl one hot afternoon. "Them mules get to rest and cool off . . . an' us hoomans got to keep on workin'."

My friend Nobie Boyles summed up the matter when he growled at the man, "You didn't cost the county a thousand bucks, you stupid bastard."

The new redhead was now struggling with a shovel at the tail end of the wagon I was loading. Even Boss Bray had sense enough to keep a new and inexperienced man out of the way of the other workers, for a shovel had a work-sharpened edge to it and could be a dangerous tool if not handled with some skill and care. Grady had brought him an old, worn shovel which would be lighter than a brand new "Four Spot," but even with this slight break the man was having rough going. Obviously he had never used a shovel in earnest before. For one thing he was shoveling cross-breasted, which would wear him out in a few hours; he was fighting the shovel instead of working with it, and the going would be rough for him until he mastered the easy, rhythmic swing that would enable him to work a fourteen- or fifteen-hour day without utterly exhausting himself. He was gripping the shovel in his white, jail-tender hands; in a few hours his palms would be raw, bleeding hamburger. The rule of silence during working hours was strictly enforced, but in spite of this, one of the more-experienced men working near him would, by whispering out of the corner of his mouth, get across to this new man the necessity of urinating on his hands. "Never waste a drop of piss!" was axiomatic among us; the only trouble was there was rarely an overabundance of this commodity. The excessive sweating in that stifling heat kept us pretty well dehydrated, and despite the fact Grady was a good water boy and passed among us with the water bucket as frequently as he could get by with it, any moisture we ingested flowed right back out through our pores. Most of us worked stripped to the waist, and when we cooled off and the sweat stopped washing our sun-blackened torsos, we would be streaked and caked with white salt dust left from the dried sweat. At least the county was unstinting in its provision of salt, and a frequent pinch of salt washed down with a dipperful of water was just one more defense in the battle for survival. A desalinized body would not hold up long doing heavy work in that heat.

During the past two years I had seen many new men come and go, and rarely did I pay much attention to them or to their sufferings. Maybe my surroundings and the conditions under which I had to live were beginning to toughen and coarsen the fibers of my being . . . I simply don't know. I knew only that I was faced with the very real prospect of spending the rest of my life in prison, for the hope of an eventual parole or pardon in my case was so remote as to be almost unthinkable. And one of the first lessons I had learned was that in prison, if you want to live, you had damned well better mind your own business. I do not know about life behind the walls of a more "civilized" penitentiary, but I do know that on a chain gang where sudden, gory, and inexplicable accidents were more or less common-place that a quick and messy end lay in wait for those who were rash enough to stick their noses into matters that did not concern them. It was too easy for a needle-sharp pick to slip from sweaty hands, or for the quick, "careless," and powerful upswing of a knife-sharp shovel edge to cut a man almost in half. And the only explanation that was required or expected was "Whoops!" That was one reason why we were rarely bothered with stool pigeons on the gangs.

During those years I had seen many new men arrive on the gang, men of varied temperament and a wide range of backgrounds, but the metamorphosis from civilian to con-vict followed a nearly identical pattern for them all. Within a few weeks these two new arrivals would make their ad-justments to this strange environment, they would gradually begin to reel in their horizons, and they would begin to learn the trick of living one day at a time. Also, as the psy-chic shock wore off, they would begin to tell others of their crimes which had landed them here and they would justify these crimes—at least in their own minds. During the twelve years I spent in prison I never once encountered a guilty man, and could one accept their initial premise, most of them were quite justified in doing whatever they had done. I used to envy my fellow convicts this bit of self-delusion which afforded them so much solace, because for me there was no such consolation. I stated earlier that there was no excuse for what I had done—neither was there reason nor explanation nor extenuating circumstances—and even the escape door of legal insanity was closed to me.

It all started one night in what was then called a "road house" on a highway leading south from Atlanta. This was during the Prohibition era, and five young men, seventeen and eighteen years old, were sitting around a table, a gallon jug of corn liquor on the table, engaged in a bull session. All of us around the table were in college, we all came from well-to-do families, and two of the families were "families of position." During the evening's discussion the subject of crime came up, which was natural enough, for the unenforce-able law of Prohibition had moved crime into the realm of big business, had got it onto an organized basis, and there was much discussion of it. As the talk continued, one boy advanced the theory that it was possible to commit the per-fect crime, that all that would be needed was organization, careful planning, and intelligence. He maintained that five people of some education, by pooling their brains and care-fully plotting and making provisions for every contingency, could very easily outwit the police, whom he contended had their hands more than full anyway. He actually made his arguments sound plausible.

Prior to that night I am certain that the idea of delib-erately setting out to commit a crime just to prove that it could be done was one of the farthest things from my mind. This held true for all the others around that table—except one.

On this particular night the young man in question had gone out to his car and, returning to the room, had placed in the center of the table a Colt .45 automatic.

"There," he said pointing to it, "is one of the ugliest weapons ever to come off the drawing boards, but it's also one of the most efficient. Just sitting there, all by itself, it looks lethal, deadly. And it's my contention that with such a weapon a determined man can be the absolute master of any situation . . ." He talked well, this young man, he talked convincingly and he hammered home his points. And he had the mysterious quality called leadership.

Starting that night five young men instigated a minor crime wave that covered a period of some weeks. A series of rapid robberies of various business establishments left the police running in circles and the newspapers screaming edi-torially for the blood of the "polite bandits." On the nights of our forays we would draw straws to determine who would enter the premises of our "cased" victim and do the actual holding up with the .45. The short straw and one other boy would travel in one car, followed by the three others in another car to block off any possible pursuit. There were several gun battles, the .45 had now drawn its first blood, and a man had been killed—but we kept on.

"We're learning," said the young man. "We're learning our trade . . . and we're proving our point. Very soon we'll wind this thing up by knocking over a bank I've been casing for some time. It'll be easy . . . and then we can quit. And we can live out the rest of our lives knowing that the perfect crime has been committed."

*   *   *

The Southern autumnal rains had started and now at eight o'clock of this October night a wind had risen and the gusts were blowing the rain in slanting sheets. The streets were slick and wet and only a few cars were out; the few pedestrians on the streets all had their collars turned up, their heads down, and were intent on getting to their destinations in a hurry. It was an ideal night for petty holdup men, muggers, and punks generally.

I had drawn the short straw this night and twice we drove past the cased target for this foray . . . a branch store of a grocery chain. Only two clerks were visible inside the store, and when the two cars stopped around the corner I stepped out, quickly walked around the corner, and with my coat collar turned up entered the store.

"This is a holdup!" I barked in as steady a voice as I could manage. "Don't move!"

The counters formed a U in the store. To my left, one of the clerks was replenishing cans on the shelves, and at the bottom of the U the other clerk was tallying up the day's receipts at the cash register. The clerk on my left slowly raised his hands, an open-mouthed look of terror on his face, but the clerk in the back—deciding to be a hero for someone else's money—snatched a revolver from under the counter and came up with it roaring fire and lead. In a reflex action I started pulling the trigger on the heavy automatic in my hand. All three of the shots I squeezed off found their target, but as the murdered victim fell across the counter he twitched off one more shot from the .38 revolver which hit me in the fleshy part of my left groin. The clerk on my left had also been killed, but even during the fusillade of shots I had seen what had happened: the hero-clerk, being unaccustomed to a hand gun, was holding the butt loosely in his palm but jerking his finger on the trigger and his shots were being pulled off to the right. It was one of these wild shots which killed the other clerk.

As I limped out to the waiting cars, I could feel the warm blood running down my leg and squishing in my shoe. The pain hadn't started yet, for the flesh was still numb from the shock of the bullet.

Right at that moment in my life I was a terrified young punk with a bullet hole in my groin out of which my blood was pouring. If I didn't die from that wound, I knew a hangman's noose was waiting for me . . . or worse yet, a prison cell for the rest of my life. But despite all this I could still feel anger—anger at a stupid clerk who thought he could shoot it out with a scared, trigger-nervous bandit who had the drop on him. If his employers had not drilled into him how to act during a holdup, the insurance companies should have. My own "initial premise" . . . ?

I was driven to the home of the young man—whose family was away on a trip—put to bed, and my wound was treated with drugstore remedies. Because of youth and those remedies, my wound healed quickly and I soon resumed my classes at Oglethorpe University. The ghastly reality and the tragic consequences of what we were doing crashed into the awareness of us all. The gun was hidden, a minor crime wave came to an abrupt halt, and five young men began to realize that what they had done in their youth would follow them to their graves.

Two weeks later the suit I had been wearing at the time of the crime turned up in a dry cleaning establishment, and because a blood-stained, bullet-holed suit is not a daily occurrence in a dry cleaner's, the police were summoned. A cleaning woman had found the suit rolled up on the floor of a closet in the young man's home. My name was in the suit and it was known from what home the suit had been sent.

I was the first to be picked up by the detectives.

"Well, well . . . what d'you know . . . a chickenshit Robin Hood we got on our hands," said Chief of Detectives Lamar as I was led into his office by two of his men. "We got certain means of getting to the truth around here." He had risen from behind his desk and was slowly slapping the palm of his hand with a length of heavy rubber hose. "I hate the sight of bruises . . . and I hate to slam people in the balls with a rubber hose. So, save me all that unhappiness, will ya? TALK!"

An hour later, after I had picked myself up off the floor for the fourth time, it seemed pointless to keep repeating like a parrot, "I have nothing to say." After all, the holes in my suit matched the holes in me . . . and there was that rubber hose.

Two hours later the young man from whose home the suit had been sent to the cleaners was picked up by the detectives. His politically powerful family had got wind of what was happening, and he was met at the old Atlanta police headquarters on Decatur Street by a prominent attorney. Chief of Detectives Lamar closed the rubber hose away in his desk drawer.

My family also moved in on the scene now, and a former United States congressman, one of the most able criminal lawyers ever to appear in a Southern courtroom, was retained to defend me. William Schley Howard assembled such a battery of legal talent to help him as had rarely been gathered in one place, and because a considerable sum of money was to become involved, the matter of my trust fund was taken before the courts. Courts are run by a closed brotherhood of lawyers, and because lawyers would benefit from the money, my trust fund was made available for my defense.

After many consultations my battery of legal talent came to the only conclusion possible: there simply was no valid and legal defense for what I had done. But because there was money available they decided to take refuge in that last defensive resort: I was to be plead "not guilty by reason of insanity."

Six respected, and high-priced, psychiatrists were retained to examine me and report their findings. The state prosecutor learned of this maneuver, and he was forced to retain six other psychiatrists whose testimony—he hoped—would offset the expected testimony of my doctors. For three weeks these twelve psychiatrists picked, probed, tested, and analyzed me, and at the end of all this mental mining they came up with two separate and final reports. They were separate reports but they both said, in effect, the same thing: I was as sane as they were.

Finally, my lawyers having exhausted all the delaying tactics at their command, I was brought to trial. For two weeks my attorneys fought manfully for my life. In a capital case the defense is not allowed to attack the law of capital punishment, but by using oblique tactics they came as close to arguing against this law as the judge would permit. These were sincere men, honest men, and they poured their hearts and their not inconsiderable minds into defending me. They made an issue of my youth, they spoke eloquently of the rewarding quality of mercy, and . . . fifteen minutes after the jury received the case the verdict was rendered: "Guilty as charged." There was no recommendation for mercy, so Judge E. D. Thomas had no alternative: ". . . until dead, dead, dead. And may God have mercy on your soul."

Then the young man was brought to trial, and because I had refused to testify against him, the prosecution basically had nothing but a very strong circumstantial case against him. After two weeks a mistrial was declared due to a hung jury. It became known that only one juror had held out for acquittal—the other eleven holding out for conviction—and his lawyers realized the heavy odds against ever finding another sympathetic juror. Facing the reality of this situation, they offered to plead their client guilty—thereby having him receive a mandatory life sentence—if I too were allowed to plead guilty and receive the same sentence. On the surface it was a grand, magnanimous gesture, but it was essentially meaningless, for my death sentence stood there as a grim roadblock to any such wheeling and dealing. This death sentence would have to be set aside before I could plead guilty, and only one man had the authority to do so.

For twenty years before his election to a judgeship on the superior court, E. D. Thomas had been a respected member of the Georgia bar. For the next twenty years he had served with distinction, honor, and bravery on the bench of the superior court of Fulton County, Georgia, and during these years his name had become synonymous with integrity. Judge Thomas was not only an honest man . . . he was a wise man. A realist.

At the time of the two trials my family could have easily raised a million dollars. The young man's family wholly owned the *Atlanta Journal*—the most powerful paper in the Southeast at that time—and millions were popcorn to them. Such money could keep two criminal cases in court until the defendants died of old age. Judge Thomas knew this.

Slowly he blew out his breath. The gavel rose and fell. ". . . and I accept the plea of guilt. It is the order of this court that these two young men spend the remainder of their natural lives in state's prison."

These kaleidoscopic thoughts flashed through my mind during the brief moment it took to bend down and scoop a shovelful of dirt onto the wagon. Although at the time of my own arrival I had been almost the same age as the younger man, I could identify more readily with the older, for I too had been bewildered and appalled by the chains and my surroundings. The older man, more experienced with life, looked like he would probably adjust more quickly to this new environment and remain less changed by this experience. But what about this malleable young boy? Society had matriculated him in one of its universities of crime, and because he was an apparent graduate of a criminal preparatory school, he would quickly learn all the lore set before him. Within two years he would learn, as I had, all that would be needed to graduate into the big time of crime. The rest would depend on his imagination and how much savvy he possessed.

The older man . . . well, if nothing else, he would learn how to pull time. With eighteen years staring him in the face he'd damned well better! But what else would he learn, and what would all these years in prison do to him? In fact, what were all these years going to do to me?

With a conscious effort I pulled my mind back from the fatal brink of this type of thinking. If I was going to emerge from the ordeal of all these years, I would have to break them down into manageable portions of twenty-four hours. With this certainty in mind I fell into the easy swing that would let me stay with the shovel for the remaining nine hours of this work day.

2.

It was undoubtedly the hat the man was wearing which had aroused my interest and piqued my curiosity in the new redhead. No one would wear such a hat under the circumstances unless there was a broad streak of perversity in his make-up; and knowing those two transfer guards, I could imagine the amount of pleading and cajoling he had put up in order to retain this civilian headgear. Apparently the hat was a sort of symbol to him, a banner nailed to his masthead, which signified—at least to himself—his determination not to let this traumatic experience beat him to the ground.

But it was more than just the hat. All of us have been in a crowded room where everyone immediately became conscious of a certain person's entrance. There is no satisfactory explanation for this phenomenon, but the new man possessed that "presence" to a remarkable degree.

My friend Nobie Boyles, the half-breed Cherokee Indian,

working in the third slot down at the end of the wagon I was loading, was next to the new man. I was glad to see that slowly, cautiously, and surreptitiously he was coaching the man in the proper handling of the unfamiliar tool. At least Nobie had got him to stop shoveling cross-breasted. It was now ten thirty and in another half hour we would stop work for the midday dinner break. During July and August we were given two hours for the dinner period. We would be marched out of the cut and over into the shade of the trees up on the bank. In fact Boss Bray was already up at the dinner site supervising Grady as the latter laid out the fifty feet of squad chain around the base of the old Chinaberry tree under which we had been eating our dinner for the past month.

At eleven o'clock Bray appeared at the edge of the cut and, throwing back his pumpkin-round head, gave forth with his unvarying mess call . . . the long, drawn out, piercing "SOOO–WEEE!" followed by the three shorter eches, "SOO–WEE, SOO–WEE, SOO–WEE!": the famous hog-slopping call of the South. Considering the food we were given, a hog-slopping call was not too inappropriate.

Dropping our tools, we formed a double line, and the shotgun men marched us out of the cut and into the blissful shade of the trees. We could smoke now, and those with cigarettes lighted up. The less fortunate made their reservations by asking a smoking friend, "Save me a drag, will ya?" Grady was waiting for us with one end of the squad chain in his hand. Under the watchful eye of Boss Bray, who was standing to one side with his hands on his hips and his round little potbelly hanging over his belt buckle, we each held out the ring on our upright chains, and Grady passed the squad chain through these rings, stringing us together like a bunch of human beads. When we were all chained together, Bray snapped a huge padlock on the end of the chain and the guards could relax at last: no one was going anywhere—at least not without taking thirty other men and a

Chinaberry tree with him. For the next two hours the rule of silence would be lifted, but most of us were too hot and tired to do much else but eat and then try to take a nap on the hard-packed bare earth.

In any group of men there is always one who is the self-appointed comedian. Ours was a man whom possibly only the South could produce. Maybe it is something in the water or in the likker, or it may be the influence of The Lost Cause, but whatever the reason, the South seems to produce these characters with alarming frequency. Our comedian, when he could stop talking long enough, answered to the name of Josh Turner. To put it bluntly, Josh was full of shit. To have heard him tell it, he was a wheeling and dealing businessman, a highly successful automobile dealer who had been framed by competitors, who envied his success. The fact of the matter, of course, was that Josh dealt in automobiles belonging to other people. The prosecutor's office finally racked up a total of fifty stolen cars against Josh, and the belief was widely held that if they hadn't gotten rather bored with the whole matter at that point, they could have gone on to a much higher score. Fifty seemed a good round figure, I suppose, and because automobile theft was a misdemeanor, Josh wound up with fifty twelve-month sentences running consecutively. But neither this, nor anything else seemed to daunt Josh, and he babbled and bubbled away as though he were to be released on the morrow.

As soon as we were all seated in a wide circle around the tree Josh, performing a daily ritual, would rise to his feet, drop his straw hat to the ground, reverently raise both arms up to the heavens, palms outstretched, and throwing back his head, would intone in a booming, sepulchral voice, "And may the Lord make our stomachs truly strong for what they are about to receive!"

All during the many months that Josh did this, Boss Bray thought the old windbag was actually offering up a solemn blessing.

Following this invocation, one of the mule skinner trusties would go around the circle handing out rusty pie pans. Each of us had his own spoon, which we carried with us in a piece of slotted leather worn on our belts. The first trusty would be followed by two others, one handing out pones of corn bread and the other forking out chunks of boiled white sow belly, which looked like translucent blobs of whale blubber. Grady would bring up the rear ladling cowpeas out of a twenty-gallon milk can. Being a Southerner, I consider black-eyed peas a delicacy, but these were not black-eyed peas; they were cattle feed. This was our unvarying menu for the midday meal. As Josh would say, "The same yesterday, and today, and forever. Amen."

Oddly enough the guards and foremen fared no better than we did in this matter of food, the only difference being that they received their peas, sow belly, and corn bread in individual dinner buckets. Boss Charlie ate his dinner seated on an up-ended dynamite box about one hundred feet away from us, and Boss Brewer, using the same type of seat, ate his dinner under another tree a hundred feet from us on the other side. Bray always ate his dinner with Brewer, for the two were old corn-likker-swilling, slattern-leching cronies. Boss Charlie always ate by himself, and I had the impression he was glad to be spared Bray's company. Charlie was several cuts in the human scale above those other two, and I often wondered what made him become a chain gang guard in the first place. But this was during the worst days of the Depression, and one worked where, how, and at what one could; with a wife and a couple of children to feed, Charlie was grateful for the three dollars a day he was being paid.

I had just begun to shovel peas into my mouth when I heard a thin, plaintive voice pipe up.

"B-B-Boss . . . Boss!" It was the newly arrived Kid, who was sitting looking down into his pan with an expression of utter dismay on his face.

"Yeah? Whatta you want?"

"B-Boss . . . there's a dead mouse in my pan!"

Without a moment's hesitation, without even a second in which to zero in his evil little mind on this problem, Boss Bray shot back at the Kid, "Gaw dann, boy . . . you ain't been here long enough to have all that meat . . . give it to one of the older men!"

There were times when Boss Bray made this show almost worth the price of admission. No matter what one's opinion of him might have been, no matter how much one may have detested him and all the evil sadism that was woven into the fabric of his being, one had to admire the quickness and the fecundity of his mind when it came to matters perverse or malevolent. I was somewhat surprised at the Kid attracting this much attention to himself and making an issue of such a trivial matter as a dead, gray, bloated mouse floating in his pan of peas. After all, it wasn't the Loch Ness monster, and furthermore, having been in a reformatory, this was probably not the first time he had encountered interesting bits of fauna floating in his pan. In fact there were many adherents to the belief that "if it doesn't bite you first, it's good to eat." Those of us who were veterans would have simply considered the mouse an unwanted garnish, like a sprig of parsley, flipped it out with our spoons, and gone on eating. But Grady did bring the Kid another ladle of peas, and we finished our dinner without further incidents.

During the summer months the hours of darkness were only too short, and I always considered the midday nap an essential part of my attempt to outlive this chain gang. But since coming onto this new project I had developed an intense dislike for that beautiful old Chinaberry tree. Its arching branches were filled with tree snakes, and Boss Bray would spend most of the two hours potshooting at the snakes with his revolver. The flat roar of that thirty-two-twenty going off at unevenly spaced intervals and the expectation of having a dead or wounded snake drop on one's head was a combination scarcely conducive to sleep.

That damned thirty-two-twenty-on-a-forty-four-frame! The way Boss Bray pronounced it, it sounded as though it was all one word, and whenever he mentioned his gun, which was frequently, his tongue seemed to lick over the words as though he were obscenely caressing them. That gun strapped up under his arm in a shoulder holster made him ten feet tall in his own eyes; to him that revolver was not just an inanimate object—it was an extension of himself and it had a heart and soul of its own. Some convict before my time— one with a smattering of the classics—had named the gun Apollyon, after the Prince of Hell in Bunyan's *Pilgrim's Progress,* and from that day to the present all the convicts in Bray's squad knew that gun, behind his back, as Apollyon. Some twelve months later when he was killed by his own gun in the hands of another, I felt sure that his last conscious thought before the steel-jacketed bullet tore into and through his brain was one of disbelief that his gun could, or would, betray him.

At ten minutes to one Bray got to his feet, settled the black felt hat on his head, and bawled out, "Awright! Le's git some work done!"

Those of us still napping were awakened by the others, and slowly—killing as much time as we could—we lined up at the two water buckets Grady had placed within the circle. This dipperful of water would have to last us for the next hour, and this moment also gave us a chance to smoke a final cigarette before going back to work.

The new redhead was standing in the line in front of me. Lightly I put my hand on his shoulder. "We got six hours to go. Take it as easy as you can . . . you'll make it."

Slowly he turned around and looked at me for a moment. Then a grin spread over his wide-mouthed, strong, ugly face.

"A friend of mine—a Roman priest—uses an expression . . . maybe I'd better borrow it. *Ni illigitimi carborundum sub.*"

"My Latin's not that good."

"Well, it's bad Latin . . . but good sense. 'Don't let the bastards grind you down.' "

I felt sure then that this man would make it. It took more than just physical toughness to weather the amount of hell the Georgia prison officials could throw at you in a casual, almost absent-minded, manner.

That afternoon was sheer, unshirted hell for Hal Heep. He was soon dripping wet with sweat, and the stiff, new striped clothing was chafing him raw in the most uncomfortable places. By four o'clock the heat and the unaccustomed toil had reduced him to a pain-racked zombie who was only on his feet through the application of massive will power. I guess the symbol of the hat, and 'ni illigitimi . . .' had much to do with it. The blisters on his hands had broken, and the blood was causing the shovel handle to stick to the flesh so that every time he lifted the shovel he suffered excruciating pain. Several times during the long afternoon Grady had appeared with a gallon can of kerosene and had poured some of this on the man's hands. Kerosene was the general panacea for all cuts and contusions on the chain gang. I was surprised that Bray allowed Grady to perform even this slight act of mercy, for the beastly, round little man had obviously taken an active dislike to this new man. It probably sprang from nothing more than the fact of his being born a Yankee. It was traditional on the gangs to allow a new man a grace period of thirty days to toughen up before he would be expected to keep up the work pace required from us older hands, but apparently Hal Heep was not to receive the benefit of this unwritten law. This tradition was not based on any charitable or merciful motive; on this particular gang it had come about because some years previously Bray, on two separate occasions, had worked new men literally to death. They had both died of heat strokes, and the warden, because of the bad publicity he had received following the second death, had forced Bray to observe this custom. Furthermore, a short while ago Robert Elliot Burns had made his escape from a camp just south of Atlanta, and the ensuing book, *I am a Fugitive from a Georgia Chain Gang,* and the more pejorative movie had stirred up a storm of protest about such brutality.

Normally a new man would be allowed to sit down for a few minutes at frequent intervals to ease his screaming muscles, but while Bray had stopped nagging and picking at him, he nevertheless refused to let Heep sit down. The poor man's only hope was simply to pass out, to keel over in his tracks, and then Bray would let a couple of us carry him over into the shade. I was expecting—and hoping—this would happen momentarily, but by seven o'clock that night when quitting time finally arrived he was staggering and barely conscious, but he was still on his feet. I have seen many instances of sheer guts in a long and misspent life, but I have rarely witnessed such a display of will power as I did that afternoon.

I suppose it is difficult for anyone to understand in these more-or-less enlightened times how a group of men could be forced to work that hard, for those hours, under those conditions. There is just one answer: fear. A quota of work was set and the pace for that work was prescribed; it was a well nigh deadly quota and pace but it was attainable and God have mercy on any poor soul who could not keep up.

Today when we see a cartoon of some hapless New England Puritan with his hands and feet fastened into stocks we find it amusing. It may have been funny in old New England, but there was nothing amusing about the stocks on a Georgia chain gang. The large, heavy wooden racks were not ordinary stocks anyway; there was a lever arrangement built into them whereby they could be raised with the culprit fastened into them. This left the poor wretch in them hanging by his wrists and ankles with several inches of clear space under his buttocks, and it took a toughness few men possess to remain in that position for more than a few minutes without crying out for mercy. I saw only one man stay in the stocks without whimpering. At the end of two hours he was released from the fiendish machine and, being unable to stand, he lay on the floor cursing his tormentors. But he was crazy anyway, so I suppose that one doesn't really count.

Also listed high in this torturer's catalogue was the sweat box, a narrow coffinlike box nailed against the side of a building. It was built so that it was impossible for a grown man to stand upright in it, and in this crouching, squeezed-in position the victim would remain for a day and a night. However, the wardens seldom used this method of punishment; it was considered too time-consuming, and there was also the undesirable result that the prisoner would be unable to work for twenty-four hours following his release.

But of all the work-inducers at the disposal of the wardens the lash was by far the most effective. A couple of years prior to my arrival the lash had been officially abolished. This act of the legislature was considered silly and ridiculous by most of the wardens in the back-country gangs, and they simply ignored the ban on the lash. The lash itself was a four-foot-long strap about three inches wide made of three thicknesses of heavy leather braded together. Because of the thickness of the leather it was almost as stiff as a board and was a terrible weapon in the hands of an angry or sadistic man. I'm thankful that I was only lashed once. This was some three months after I had arrived at this camp. One day Bray seemed to feel that a lashing might do me good, just on general principles. The warden was the official lasher, and that night when we arrived back at the camp my shirt was stripped off, and I was handcuffed to a post that stood before the office. The whole camp was lined up and forced to witness the fate of this particular transgessor. The warden, stepping back a couple of paces, wound up and let fly with the lash across my shoulders. To this day I can still vividly remember counting those five strokes and bracing myself against each one. The first blow knocked me to my knees, and that was the position in which I took the other four. Any man who could do this to a fellow human being was probably doing more spiritual damage to his own soul than he was doing physical harm to the person he was lashing. But there was small comfort in that thought at the time.

That night when we got back to the camp Nobie and I helped Hal Heep get washed up at the trough, and then, with one of us on each side of him, we helped him into the steaming, sweat-reeking mess shack. Nobie and I and several of the others had worked out an arrangement with one of the neighboring farmers whereby he would deliver milk to us every evening, so while Heep was unable to eat, we at least got a couple of big tin cupfuls of milk into him. He had just finished the last of his milk when the cup dropped from his torn hands, and he pitched face forward on the greasy table, out cold. Picking him up, we carried him over to our cage where there was an empty bunk, and in the light of the lantern we put him down. We took off his shirt, loosened his belt, and while I was removing the heavy new brogans from his feet, Nobie went out and brought back a towel he had soaked in cold water at the pump. Laying this across Heep's forehead, he stepped back and stood silently for a moment, looking down at the man. Slowly shaking his head, he echoed the thought that was going through my mind. "The poor bastard."

From under one of the bunks we pulled out a length of old harness leather we had got hold of some time before and set to work with our knives making a pair of leg belts for this new man. He would need these garters to hold the shackles up high on his legs in order to give himself as much stride as possible and also to keep the stride chain from dragging and tripping him. In the morning I would tear two strips off an old blanket and show him how to wrap these around his ankles so that the shackles would not rub the flesh and cause shackle sores. Anyone who contracted a shackle sore got short sympathy from the warden, for it was considered an act of carelessness, and there was always the suspicion that the wound might be self-inflicted.

As we were working on the leg belts Jack Travis came in from the mess shack, and swinging himself up into his top bunk, sat silently watching us for a moment or two.

"How come you two guys are takin' so much pains with this new joker? What's he to you two?"

"Look, Travis," Nobie replied slowly, continuing to notch out the belt, "I know you think every new man's a fink until he proves different. Well, somehow I just feel this guy might be worth helping. So, belt up, ya stir crazy bastard. An' go to sleep. Okay?"

Mumbling something about Boy Scouts, Travis rolled over in his bunk and was soon snoring. There were few men on that gang who would have talked to Travis in this manner, Travis was considered the most dangerous man in the camp. Probably the sight of that razor-sharp knife in Nobie's hand even more than his six-feet-four-inch frame caused Travis to think better of starting an argument over nothing. During the year he had been in this camp he had already been involved in six knife fights, and most of them had been serious ones. And Nobie was right: slowly, surely, and inevitably the man was going stir crazy; he had spent most of his thirty-five years in various prisons, and his current offense, twenty years for armed robbery, had been carried out while he was on parole from Kilby prison in Alabama. So, even if he lived out his twenty years in Georgia, he would be returned to Alabama to face more years in prison, and he was painfully aware of the brutal fact that only through escape would he ever again know freedom. The guards too realized this and never for a moment did they give him a chance.

Certainly any man in prison lives on hope; no matter how grim the present, he has to believe in the very depths of his being that tomorrow things will be better. Hope is the one dream, the Holy Grail, that allows him to retain his sanity; slam this door of hope, and his mind, rebelling at reality, slowly fades off into the swirling mists and fogs of buffering unreality. This was now happening to Travis, and while he had probably always been of an antisocial nature, he was now becoming as vicious and dangerous as a wounded animal. For some reason both Nobie and I got along well enough with Travis. There was the undeniable fact that Nobie and I had certain reputations in this jungle, which Travis perhaps, even in his fogged thinking, respected. But toward me I think Travis felt a real sense of friendship, or at least as much of that emotion as such a man is capable of feeling. This had come about through an incident that occurred earlier that year; it happened on April first and I remember thinking at the time that Boss Bray probably considered it an April Fools' joke.

Grady had just begun to make one of his rounds with the water bucket, and I was the first man he got to. Out of the corner of his mouth he whispered to me, "Apollyon's unloaded. Tell the rest of 'em."

Grady had no more than got this warning out of his mouth when Bray climbed down from the bank and stood a few feet in front of us; Travis was working next to me and I was unable to get the message even to him, much less the rest of the gang. Bray had a bucket of stiff mud in his hand and was ostensibly preparing a dobied dynamite charge on top of a huge boulder we had unearthed the day before. We had shoveled the dirt away from this rock, and a half-stick of dynamite packed on top of it with mud would shatter it into pieces small enough for us to load onto the wagons. Bray had removed his revolver from its shoulder holster and had stuck it into his hip pocket; there was nothing suspicious about this, for he often did this in order to get it out of his way when he had some task to perform. But what was suspicious was the fact that he had never before got this close to Travis, and now here he was, ten feet in front of us, bent over the rock with the butt of the revolver dangling invitingly in front of Travis. I shot a quick glance upward at Boss Brewer standing on the bank, and I was reminded of a cat standing motionless before a rat hole, every fiber and hair of his being tensed for the kill. Brewer had the brim of his black felt hat pulled down, shading his eyes, and he was holding the shotgun with the stock up against his right hip so that a quick flip would put the gun in firing position. Immediately I saw how the whole plot was intended to work: Travis would make one leap and get his hands on the gun, then Bray would simply fall over on the other side of the boulder, and Travis would be standing out in the clear snapping an empty gun at Brewer. There would be a routine, haphazard grand jury investigation of the killing, but it would be an open and shut case, for God help any convict stupid enough to testify that the revolver was unloaded. It was a neat, murderous plan, and it would certainly get Travis out of the way once and for all. I knew that the twelve gauge shotgun Brewer carried had a choke barrel, but even with that it was quite likely that the outer rim of the cone of fire would bracket me. It did not seem that I had much to live for, but I had no desire to die in that fashion.

Next to me I could sense Travis gathering his heavy muscles and getting set for his leap. And then, just as he dropped his shovel and started the leap, with my left hand I shot the blade of my shovel between his ankles. As I knew it would, his leap fell several feet short of Bray, and he sprawled in the dust with his powerful hands clutching out for Bray's ankles. Bray leaped over behind the rock and immediately saw what had happened.

"What the hell's the matter with ya, ya bastard?" he snarled at Travis.

"I tripped," said Travis, pulling himself to his feet. Brewer now had the shotgun to his shoulder, and it was a second or two before he lowered it and I started breathing again.

"Yeah, ya tripped all right," sneered Bray. "I know what ya was tryin' to do. Now git back to work, ya son of a bitch!"

Climbing back up on the bank, Bray disappeared for a few moments but he was soon back standing next to Brewer. Apollyon was now back in its holster and had undoubtedly been reloaded. The two were standing close together, and I could see Brewer talking to him in low tones, gesturing with his free hand; I was sure he was explaining to Bray just how I had thrown a monkey wrench—or shovel, rather—into his cute little plot, and I knew that sooner or later, somehow, somewhere, someday he would make me pay dearly for fouling up his scheme. This was something I could look forward to with certainty, for Bray was not one to forget an act such as this.

That night when we returned to camp and I had just finished washing up at the trough, Travis came up to me and hesitantly began, "George, I . . . uh, . . . well, I want to thank ya . . . well, ya see, Grady just told me Apollyon was unloaded . . ."

Wrapping the towel around my neck, I just grinned at him and walked over to the mess shack. What was there to say to the man? After all I had probably saved my own life as well as his. But from that moment there developed the strange friendship that Travis seemed to feel for me. However, I knew that his fuse was getting shorter and shorter and that before long the inevitable explosion had to take place.

Soon the last of my cage mates returned from his supper, and just before falling into his iron bunk, he extinguished the lantern hanging from the top of the cage. I lay for some time in the darkness and the sweltering heat of the cage and tried to turn off the thought processes that were blocking the restorative sleep that I badly needed, but no matter how hard I tried to turn my mind into a blank, my thoughts kept hammering back at me. I could hear the regular breathing and soft snoring of the other men, but Hal Heep, lying in the bunk across from mine, was moaning softly in his tortured dreams. Apparently on this night he was not even to find relief in the balm of sleep. After a while, buckling my belt and holding my chains up by the upright so as not to disturb the others with my clanking, I padded out into the compound in my bare feet. I knew I had a few more minutes before two of the night guards, armed only with flashlights, would enter the compound, do a bunk check, and then slam and lock the cage doors for the rest of the night. Not the least of the many ordeals of prison life is the fact of never being able to be alone, of never being out of sight or hearing of other human beings, and that was why I always treasured these few brief moments every night when, standing out under the stars, I could be as near to being alone as possible. The barbed-wire fence was dimly lighted by electric lamps hanging from poles at intervals along the length of wire. The only power the camp had was furnished by a Delco system which provided just sufficient light for the night guards to see what they had to see. In the dim and uncertain light I could see their wraithlike figures slowly patrolling outside the fence with shotguns cradled in their arms. Turning my face up, I looked into the star-filled heavens. The stars were singularly large and close on this soft August night, and the gentle breeze dried the sweat on my forehead. It was quiet and peaceful out there, and by looking up one could almost forget one's surroundings; but for some reason I was unable to shake off the strange depression that had gripped me earlier in the evening. Looking up at those cold impersonal stars, I remember becoming filled with an unaccustomed bitterness and I cursed God. How could a God of mercy torture one man until he was driven to the brink of madness? How could a God of kindness do to another man that which had been done to Hal Heep this day? And how could a God of justice allow to exist such an affront to the human soul as this chain gang and its Boss Bray? For some moments I stood there thus, and finally the bitterness drained from me; it was as though my cursing had acted as a cathartic on my soul, and returning to the cage, I lay down on my bunk and was soon engulfed in the sleep of exhaustion.

3.

This book is not anything if it is not a paean
to the indomitableness of the human spirit.
And here I am not speaking of my own personal spirit, for
too often, in moments of crisis or when faced with seemingly impossible odds, it came close to wilting; instead, I am
speaking in broad terms of that unquenchable inner flame
which pervades the entire human race. And never in a long
life have I ceased to be amazed by its tenacity. At times it
may waver, it may burn down to a spark, but, short of
death, it will flare up again and blaze forth with an even
greater brilliance, lighting up the dark corners of men's
souls and making us all proud of our human heritage.

History is filled with examples of this resoluteness of the
human spirit. The carving out of the brave state of Israel
in the face of impossible odds, the guts and endurance of
Ernest Gordon and his fellow British captives in the notor-
ious Japanese prison camp on the River Kwai: these are two

of the spectacular examples, the ones that make the head-lines. But what of the quiet man who goes about the daily task of just living, who performs those obligations which are duty-bound on us all, who just carries out the routine, often boring, processes of his daily life without fanfare and yet, through it all stays reasonably cheerful and brings a share of happiness to those who love and depend on him. To me this quiet man is the real unsung hero of the human epic. And his is the type of courage I lack.

All during the black days of the chain gang I saw ex-amples of this quiet courage, evidence of this inexhaustible human spirit. I saw it in men who, having made a ghastly mess of their lives at one point, quietly worked out their time and returned to life on the outside to resume their duties as law-abiding citizens. They were the ones who re-fused to listen to the old prison adage: "You can never come back!" This low blow to the gut of hope is hatched and kept alive by the two- (or more) time losers who have gone out, made a halfhearted effort at going straight, become dis-heartened at their first rebuff, and slid back into a life of crime as the easy out. No ex-convict can ever turn back the hands of the clock. His record is there indelibly, and he has to live with it. The key to the whole problem lies in the word *acceptance:* all of us have to accept things that we simply cannot change, otherwise there is little chance for happiness, balance, or sanity.

Perhaps a solution to this problem of human entrapment lies in the prayer attributed to Reinhold Niebuhr:

> God grant me the serenity
> To accept the things I cannot change,
> Courage to change the things I can
> And wisdom to know the difference.

One of the great drawbacks to life in prison is that, nec-essarily, one's choice of friends is limited. I was fortunate to have during my twelve years a few friends who were really outstanding men, men who had in common this calm acceptance, a quiet courage, and an unquenchable spirit.

A few in this group still stand out vividly in my memory. There was Nobie Boyles—twenty to forty years for armed robbery—six feet four inches tall, high cheek bones, black, straight hair, half Cherokee Indian. He simply saw nothing wrong in taking anything he wanted from other people. That, after all, was what his father's people had done to his mother's people. And yet he was a man with an unflinching code of ethics and a loyal friend. Despite Nobie's peculiarly Indian—and in my mind, justified—attitude toward this life, he came to realize this is a white man's hypocritical world and he would have to live with and accept it. Nobie was determined to work out his time and try for a parole, and I felt certain that on his release he would never return to prison.

There was Uncle Billy Jones, a peterman, a safe-cracker serving thirty years—five feet six inches tall and in his early sixties. He had a pointed face like a fox, twinkling eyes, gray hair, and a frame made of rawhide and piano wire. When he moved and one saw the youthful, muscular manner in which he handled himself, one realized the gray hairs and the lines in his face were all on the surface, like nicks on a granite boulder. He had spent over half his life in reformatories and prisons. Had life been kinder to him, I am sure he would have been an M. I. T. professor, for at heart he was a frustrated mechanical engineer. Even an unopened can of sardines was a challenge to him. But Billy had a morbid fear of dying in prison, and I saw the great change come over him following the visit of a younger brother. This man had made a fortune in the citrus fruit business in Florida and he now wanted to help his erring brother: he hired two lawyers and supplied the money that would be needed to properly present Billy's case before the parole board when he became eligible. For the first time in his life Billy began to live with hope. I felt certain that in the future Billy would content himself with opening sardine tins—and not other people's Mosler safes.

But of all the men who were my friends during those years, it is undoubtedly Hal Heep who was the most outstanding. The name he used was an alias, and none of us ever knew his true name. It came to light that he was an unfrocked Jesuit priest who had been laicized because he was suffering from a disease that later came close to laying me by the heels—alcoholism. Through this friend I was able to continue with my education, which had been brought to an abrupt halt by my own stupid actions. For almost four years he tutored and taught me, supervised my reading, probed and picked at my mind, and made me think. During those four years I am sure I learned more from him than I would have in college. I owe many people in this world many things, but to Hal Heep I owe a debt that can never be paid. I just hope that I, by keeping his mind occupied, helped him to withstand the horrors that besieged his life during those years.

The physical effects of his long years of alcoholic drinking were thrown off in a relatively short time due to the work, the sweating, and the rough, simple food. But it took many months for the alcoholic thinking to be worked out of his mind. However, eventually this did happen, and almost from day to day I could witness the miracle of this metamorphosis. For one thing, now that he could again think with some clarity, he realized that the only enemy he had in this world was alcohol. I knew little about alcoholism in those days, and I do not think I really understood him when he talked of the irresistible compulsion that flooded through him when he took even so much as one drink. Later on I came to know personally and to dread that awful compulsion only too well. But there was something about Heep which made me feel certain that now that he had his disease arrested (there is no "cure" for this disease), he would never again take that first drink. He himself was the first to acknowledge that this prison experience had been a blessing to him in this respect. His religion meant much to him, and the most shattering and traumatic thing that had ever occurred to him had been his laicizing. He carried the hope in the depths of his being that he could someday, somehow, regain his priestly status. It would be a long road, he would probably have to start out as a lay brother, but the hope never died within him that eventually he would attain this goal.

Prison time monotonously crept by, and after a couple of months Heep, due to his own dauntless spirit and what help the rest of us could give him, had weathered the worst part of his experience. His outwardly frail appearance contrasted with his wiry and resilient physique, and it was amazing how quickly he adapted to this rough, tough mode of life. Even Travis, to my surprise, and begrudgingly at first, took a liking to the man and did what he could to help him.

By now the Kid had made "her" choice and had accepted Bub Fletcher as her unlawfully wedded husband. There had been neither rice nor old shoes nor had anyone baked a cake, but they seemed quite happy and had moved into a cage with four other wedded couples. Bub was calf-eyed over his bride, and at least there had been no knife fights during the courtship.

Most normal people feel a certain revulsion toward homosexuality, but, as I said earlier, it is a matter of complete indifference to me what two consenting adults do between them. Under the conditions I think such a situation was inevitable, and I could understand it—and condone it. This was a brutal, harsh life we lived, and we were surrounded on all sides by violence, sadism, and horror. As a partial escape from this atmosphere it was natural that a friendship would spring up between individuals with more or less similar tastes; and love would eventually develop from these friendships. These relationships invariably took place between an older man and a younger one, and I have seen grow between such couples a genuine affection, an amount of unselfishness, a tenderness, and a high respect for each other that is too often missing in normal marriages. From such a friendship two men found kindness, an understanding of each other, and a surcease from the unremitting brutality and coarseness of their environment. As a matter of course these two would share between them whatever small luxuries one of them would happen on; if one of them was able occasionally to obtain a bit of "outside" food with which to relieve the dull monotony of the daily fare, he would make certain his mate got his share, and it was always the choicer or larger share. If one of them fell sick or was injured, the other would nurse him with care that is not to be found in the best of hospitals. In two separate instances I have seen one give up smoking in order that his mate could have his weekly ration of Golden Grain tobacco, and in both cases the one making the sacrifice did so quietly, without fanfare.

When I first arrived on the chain gang I was eighteen years old and what novelists would call "a clean-limbed youth"; so I suppose it was inevitable that I should run full tilt into this form of sexual aberration and that the wolves would take an interest in me. The same Bub Fletcher who later married the Kid was especially attentive to me, doing me little favors, giving me bits of advice, and generally trying to ingratiate himself to me. I was young but not so naive as to be blind to what he had in mind, and at that time I could think of no way of discouraging him and making him realize once and for all that I just was not interested in what he intended. I could not very well use the words of the girl in the dime novel: "Oh, sirrah . . . your intentions are not honorable!" but I had to find some way of ending this. I was still puzzling over this problem when the whole pot boiled over one Saturday afternoon after we had bathed and been issued fresh clothing. Approaching me, he began in an oblique manner to present his proposition and then came out with it in plain words. Had I been older and more experienced, I would have simply laughed at him, probably thanked him for his "generous offer," and let him know civilly and firmly that I was not interested. Instead, for one of the few times in my life, I lost my temper and in plain, four-letter words told him what I thought of him and his proposition and told him graphically what he could do with this proposal. Before my eyes the great love that he had just been professing turned into hate—or a very good facsimile of it—and the next thing I knew, this great bearlike man was rushing me. He had huge hairy arms like a gorilla's, and I knew that if he ever got those arms around me he could crush my whole rib cage easily. The only way I could fight this brute was to keep sidestepping his rushes and let him wear himself out, so remembering everything I had ever been taught about self-defense I easily side-stepped his first rush and whirled around, getting set for the next rush. By now the entire camp had formed a circle around us and was silently watching this sport. I knew I would get no help from any of them, for it was part of this jungle's code that no one would interfere in a fight. Not, at least, until one of the combatants was rendered helpless. Then they would step in and stop it. When I turned to face him for the second rush he had lowered his head and was glaring at me from under his brows, and strange animal noises were gurgling out of his throat. He came at me with his arms flailing wildly. Again, at the last moment I sidestepped him, but this time as his momentum carried him past me I brought the edge of my extended right hand down across the side of his neck in a wicked chopping motion. It was a vicious blow that would have loosened the brain of a lesser man, but it simply knocked him to his knees, where he remained for a moment or two shaking his head to clear it and growling. He was soon on his feet and coming at me again. I was amazed that he did not change his tactics, but apparently these bull-like rushes had always served him victoriously in the past, and he could not believe that they were going to fail him now. Three more times he tried the same thing and three more times I chopped him to his knees. The last one finished him; remaining on his knees and again shaking his head to get his wits back in place, he slowly looked up at me. The hate was gone from his face now, replaced by a look bordering on awe, or wonder. Then, still on his knees, he threw back his head and started roaring with laughter. After a moment he got control of himself and, wiping his streaming eyes, looked up at me with a great grin spread across his face.

"By God, George," he laughed, "you whupped me fair an' square . . . an' you're the fust man to do that since I was ten years old. Between the two of us we could whup this whole goddam camp. Come here, shake my hand and ho'p me up."

I'm not sure what reaction I had expected from the man but it certainly was not this one. Warily, still suspecting a trick of some kind, I walked over to him and helped him to his feet. Throwing one of those gorilla arms around my shoulders, he let out a screeching rebel yell and boomed, "By God, you ain't no punk . . . you're a man!" I am happy—and proud—to say that from that day on Bub Fletcher and I were good friends.

Shortly after the fight with Bub there occurred an incident that is less to my credit. Some time after my arrival a man whose time had expired presented me with a cake of unused Lifebuoy soap on the morning of his release. The soap provided by the county was a harsh, yellow lye laundry soap, and while it effectively removed the dirt, there was some risk that it would also remove the skin of the user, so this cake of "store-bought" soap represented a minor treasure in these circumstances. For two days, morning and night, I luxuriated in my new gift, and then on the third day my treasure disappeared. Two days later it suddenly appeared one night at the wash trough in the hands of a fellow convict. This man was a peculiar sort of person, even in an environment where peculiar people were rather commonplace; he was a loner who rarely opened his mouth to anyone, and he had no friends and seemed to want none. One had the impression that the snarl of an animal was just beneath his surface. He had been committed under an alias, and while he had the telltale marks of a man who has become thoroughly institutionalized, his fingerprints strangely revealed nothing about him. He had been arrested and sentenced to six to ten years for having run amuck, apparently for no good reason, one afternoon in the men's room in the basement of the Piedmont Hotel in Atlanta. Whipping out a knife, he had suddenly started slashing at people and had cut one man severely before he had been subdued. Obviously he was as mad as a hatter and never should have been sent to prison. In an institution for the criminally insane he might have received the help he needed.

But I knew none of this on this particular night; I knew only that he had taken my soap, that he was using it defiantly, openly, in an apparent gesture of contempt, and that the whole chain gang was a witness to this patent taunting.

Going up to where he was bending over the wash trough, I tapped him on his bare shoulder. "Friend," I said evenly, "if you can prove you bought that soap, it's yours. But I happen to think that's my soap. "

He didn't say anything, nor did he turn around or straighten up. Slowly he put the soap on the side of the trough, reached out for a filthy towel, and carefully dried his hands. Then in one swift rush of movement he whirled around, still in a crouch. His hand flashed to his hip pocket and reappeared with a switchblade knife. With his thumbnail he flipped open the evil-looking blade and with a roundhouse, looping righthand swing he slashed at my midriff. Had he known how to use that knife, had he thrust straight in, low and upward, I would have been defenseless; but his clumsy, looping swing gave me the split second I needed to jump back and suck in my stomach. As his hand flashed by my stomach I brought the edge of my right hand down on his wrist. The knife flew out of his hand and, much quicker than it takes to tell, it was in mine. In an almost reflex action I thrust inward with the blade, in and low and up. I felt it go home up to my wrist, I heard the breath go out of him in a loud "whoosh," and his body sagged to the ground.

The guards outside the fence knew that something had happened, the warden was summoned, and in a few minutes, accompanied by three guards, he entered the compound. "Aw right!" he bellowed. "What happened? Who done it?" Fifty men had seen the incident—but there was not a witness among the lot. Fifty men were busily engaged in washing at the trough . . . and the body lay sprawled in the red dust.

"Ya gawdanned convicts!" the warden roared after a moment of this silence, his frustration and anger boiling over. "That's why you're in here . . . ya ain't got no gawdanned sense o' civic dooty!" After shouting this pronouncement he spun on his heel and strode toward the gate, accompanied by the three guards.

For an hour the body lay there and no one went near it. (There was no doubt the man was dead.) And then two Negro trusties, carrying shovels, a lantern, and a blanket, came in, wrapped the body in the blanket, and carried it out the gate. With one of them carrying the shrouded body over his shoulder and the other carrying the shovels and the lantern, they disappeared into the woods which surrounded the camp, and the bobbing of the lantern was the sole requiem for this strange, unknown, lost soul whose life I had ended in a burst of violence. He was simply buried in an unmarked grave and forgotten, and his name was stricken from the records.

Had circumstances been different and had I been taken into a court of law with witnesses, I undoubtedly could have proved self-defense and I would have been acquitted. But there is something more to life than mere legality, and I knew then—and have known ever since—that what I did that night was not in defense of my life. What I did I did out of sheer cowardice. I was afraid, afraid of what my fellow convicts would think of me if I let that poor, demented man get by with stealing a ten-cent cake of soap from me; I was afraid and to cover my fear I put on a cheap grandstand play. A man died because I was afraid—afraid of what people with warped values would think of me.

It's a sad commentary on the state of mind of my associates of those days, but my cheap, fear-inspired, bloody act of that night redounded to my benefit. From then on, I was known as a "killer"—a man who would brook no interference in his private affairs—and no one ever again stole a ten-cent cake of soap from me.

4.

Later on in the afternoon of my fight with
Bub Fletcher I was at the wash trough trying
to launder some of the red grime out of my towel when
Nobie Boyles approached me. Grinning, he slipped something into my pocket.

"It's an extra one I had," he said. "It doesn't look like
you'll ever need it . . . but it's good to have, just in
case . . ."

It was a wicked-looking hawk-billed clasp knife. This
was the first time Nobie had spoken to me, but I realized
that through the presentation of this illegal knife he was
extending his friendship to me. Knives were contrary to all
prison regulations, and from time to time the guards would
hold a search operation and confiscate basketfuls of them,
but within a few weeks everyone would again have a knife.
But they were hard to obtain, and I was fully aware of the
value and the meaning of this gift.

The next day, Sunday, was visiting day, and one of the first visitors to arrive—as she did every visiting day—was the gorgeous, suntanned blonde who came to see Tom Coughlin, one of Nobie's cage mates. She always arrived in a blue La-Salle touring car with the top down, and she was an eye-filling sight. I may have been just a sex-starved punk in those days, but that woman was one of the most strikingly beautiful women I had ever seen. Even the atrocious, flat-breasted, low-waisted styles that were modish in those days could not hide the fact that this blonde was all woman. And the fact that she worshipped Tom could be felt, almost like an electric shock. Visitors were allowed to come up just to the single strand of barbed wire some ten feet outside the fence of the compound. It must have been sheer agony for Tom to be that close to this embodiment of beautiful, eager love without being able to at least clasp her in his arms. She never failed to bring his a large hamper of home-cooked food, usually fried chicken and potato salad and stuffed eggs and cake and . . . that hamper seemed bottomless. She would have to leave this at the office, where one of the guards would search it before bringing it to the gate and giving it to Tom. I had noticed that the men with whom Tom shared his cage had erected a crude table just outside the cage, and every Sunday visiting day, after visiting hours were over, they would spread out whatever food any of them had received, and all of them would share in the feast. This camp was a long way from Atlanta, and my mother, sister, and brother had not yet worked out a feasible, or even possible, means of getting down to see me; so, from a distance, I would covertly watch these lucky ones down all that delicious food.

I can still remember the gratitude I felt on this particular Sunday following my fight with Bub when Tom Coughlin came up to me and said, "George, come on over and join us . . . we got plenty of food for another mouth."

They not only had food but also a tin gallon can of raw

corn whiskey, smuggled in to them by one of the trusties. Several healthy jolts of this and all that good food brought me about as close to nirvana as I could get without having a full pardon in my pocket.

And then on the following Saturday, after the bath ritual, Tom and Nobie came over and suggested that I move into their cage, where there was an empty bunk. Now I knew I had arrived, for I had been accepted by those who had the reputations of being the most "solid cons" on that gang. Many warm and wonderful things have happened to me in a long life; I remember the good moments, the open hand of friendship, the word of encouragement during a bleak period of dispair, the smile, the nod of approval. But never before, nor since has the extension of friendship meant to me what it did on that Saturday afternoon so many years ago. That response can never be the same—for the framework can never be duplicated.

I had been sharing a cage with seven short-termers, and I was filled with apprehension that in very short order they would turn me into a babbling idiot. For one thing, every one of them kept a calendar prominently displayed on which they, with great gloating, would mark off the exact number of days remaining in their sentences. The cage was also constantly filled with chatter about what would be the first things they would do when released.

"Man, I'm goin' to git me a room full of nekkid women . . . an' I'm goin' to grease them gals, an' then I'm goin' to squirm and wiggle and wriggle my way through that whole room . . ."

Even after the passage of all these years that remains in my mind as the epitome of . . . I'm not sure just what. Anyway, it was with a great sense of release that I gathered up what few belongings I had and moved in with my new cage mates. For the most part, these were older and more mature men, not necessarily from the standpoint of years, but certainly more mature and wise in the tricks of pulling time successfully than had been the chattering short-termers. These men had learned long ago that when a group of men lives closely confined, any constant nattering can be a nerve-scraping irritant, and so there was little unnecessary conversation in this cage. All of them seemed to have developed the reading habit, and as there were no restrictions on reading material, there was an ample supply of books and magazines. I have always believed that a human being could withstand almost anything if he were just allowed to read, and as I tossed my gear onto the bunk I made a promise to myself that someday I would get through the whole pile of books I noticed in one end of the cage.

As I got to know these men better I came to realize that of the eight of us five—Nobie, Uncle Billy, Jim Barfield, Jerry Klein, and I—were prepared to grant that society's laws were bigger and tougher than we were, that we were on the sucker end of the deal, and that we had better accept the fact. Technically all of us were eligible for parole after serving three years, but for lifers, such as Jim Barfield and I, parole after only three years was unheard of. Both Jim and I knew this, we knew that we would have to serve at least ten years before we could even start dreaming of freedom, and we were prepared to do so.

Jim Barfield was another of those men whose image will always stay fresh in my mind. He was an uncomplicated man, a decent, honest mountain man from the north Georgia hills of Rabun County who had killed a man for stealing his still. Jim was, of course, "innocent"; he had killed in order to protect his means of livelihood and the welfare of his wife and three children. It's all in the point of view. Also Jim was among that select group of men I have known who are completely illiterate. I say "select," for such men invariably possess a compensating shrewdness, and Jim had this to an amazing degree. He knew that to progress in this world of "readin' and writin'" he would have to learn to do just that, and he was determined to make these prison

years supply him with the education outside life had denied
him.

In Jerry Klein he found his cicerone into this wilderness
of the written word. Jerry was a quick-minded, perverse-
humored confidence man who had decided to serve out his
four years rather than try for the dubious "freedom" of escape, and almost as a challenge he took on the education of
Jim Barfield. The textbook they used was an old battered
edition of the King James Version of the Bible, and after
three years Jim Barfield probably was the only man in the
twentieth century who wrote perfect Elizabethan English.
At times, remembering his "education," he even spoke that
way. It could be disconcerting.

Two of the men in the cage had a limited amount of
money they could call on, and two of the others had friends
and relatives on the outside who kept them supplied with
moderate amounts of cash. After my fiasco I was now broke.
That, of course, is a relative expression, for despite the fact
I had paid off—for twice the amounts asked—two "murder"
lawsuits, had paid off a battery of lawyers and six psychiatrists, I still had a handful of dollars in my tattered trust
fund. My brother was the custodian of this corporal's guard
of cash, and once a month he was able to send me a small
check. The rules specified that no convict could have on his
person more than two dollars at a time. Any money in excess
of this was kept in his account in the warden's office. The
trick was to draw as often as possible the allowable two
dollars and hoard the surplus in the tin Prince Albert cans
in which we all carried our sweat-damageable possessions.
At that time the Great Depression was chewing the ass out
of the dollar: name brand cigarettes were fifteen cents a
pack—two packs for a quarter—"store" bread was five cents
a loaf, and milk was ten cents a quart. With values such as
these we were able to raise our living standard above the
just-bearable.

My friend Bub Fletcher was one of the unfortunates who

had no one on the outside to send him even a dime, but somewhere in his wild career he had picked up the ability to cut a reasonable head of hair. I was able to buy a set of barber tools and set him up in business, with the understanding that my haircuts would be on the house. From then on, every Saturday afternoon and Sunday Bub was a busy man with a waiting list of customers and, charging fifteen cents a haircut, he and his bride were now living well.

Soon I discovered that my new cage mates were able to keep on hand at all times a communal supply of corn whiskey; it was five dollars a gallon, and the trustie who smuggled it in got two dollars. We shared this weekly expense among us. Most of us in the cage got in the habit of taking a big slug of this raw, green liquor every morning as soon as we finished brushing our teeth and washing up at the trough. Every morning, except Sunday, when the new day was just a gray suspicion in the east we were awakened by one of the guards beating on a large triangular piece of steel that hung by the front gate. That ringing, clanging cacophony would have aroused twelve hells, and more racket ensued as some two hundred and forty men arose and clanked around with loose chains on iron floors. This in itself was an unholy way to start a day, but add to this the prospect of facing that unvarying, God-abandoned breakfast, and any man would have found justification for that early morning drink—at least it seemed to make the breakfast a bit more palatable. The guards and the warden knew of this flow of whiskey into the camp, but they turned their heads, and we knew this indulgence would continue just as long as no incidents arose from it. After all, they were only being paid three or four dollars a day . . . and they too had to live. Later on, after Hal Heep had joined us and after I had learned about him and his problem, I was glad to see that he never took even one drink, although he could have helped himself anytime.

Heep's first summer drew to a close, and then the cool days of autumn passed on, and we got into the winter season of rain and raw weather. It never got really cold down there in south Georgia, but during the rainy season there was a constant dampness in the air that soaked into the bones. The county supplied old pieces of ripped tarpaulins with which we could drape the outside of the cages, and each cage had a charcoal burner that did some good against the raw air; but winter was still a miserable time, for the iron roofs and floors sweated constantly and the blankets always felt damp and clammy. At least the work day was short, and on many days, because of the relentless rains, we were not even taken out to work. It was during this period that Heep began tutoring me and continuing my education. He drew up an outline of study and made a list of books I would need initially. I sent this list on to my brother, who procured the books for me. During this period Mr. Miller of Miller's Book Store in Atlanta was especially helpful, for many of these books had to be traced down and specially ordered.

Heep first questioned me extensively and tested my absorbtion of the subjects I had studied in boarding school and college; then, seemingly satisfied with my educational progress up to that point, he chartered the course for future studies. From then on, almost every day, I would read and try to absorb that which he had outlined for me. Afterwards we would have long periods of discussion during which he would give his views on the matters about which I had been reading. On Saturday afternoons or Sundays, weather permitting, we would carry on these discussions while slowly walking around in the compound, shuffling along with our heads lowered and our hands behind our backs, our chains clanking. But on rainy days we would sit on my lower bunk and hold our discussions in lowered voices so as not to disturb the others in the cage. After a while I noticed that some of the others began joining these discussions, sitting for the most part in rapt attention, occasionally asking a pertinent question. Two who more regularly joined in were Tom and Nobie.

Heep's misfortune was my good fortune. The man was a born teacher. He had that talent, or knack, which is the hallmark of a good teacher but which is too often missing in those of that profession: the ability to instill in a pupil a large measure of intellectual curiosity. Learning became an exciting adventure. Ever since those days I have been aware of how much I owe Hal Heep, and while in a material sense I have never made much of what he taught me, at least my enjoyment of life has been greater.

In my memory I treasure an incident that occurred one late March morning of that year. It must have been 1930. It was Sunday, and it was one of those days that God can occasionally produce when He really puts His mind to the job. For the first time that year the sun was bright and warm and carried within it the sure promise that winter was over. Also for the first time that year the birds were singing, and the radiance and freshness of the new day made one glad to be alive, no matter what the circumstances. My cage mates and I had acquired several cans of salmon the day before, and the cooks, for a share in the feast, had made salmon balls and some decent gravy for our breakfast and had toasted a loaf of store bread. We even had an egg apiece for that memorable meal. We were sitting on empty dynamite boxes outside the cage, smoking the first after-breakfast cigarette and soaking up the sun's warm rays when Heep, leaving the mess shack, walked up to us. He stood in front of us for a moment and then in his rich, priestly voice began quoting: " 'For, lo, the winter is past, the rain is over and gone; the flowers appear on the earth; the time of the singing of birds is come, and the voice of the turtle is heard in our land.' "

To me the Song of Solomon has always been one of the most beautiful pieces of literature ever written in any language, but Heep's beautiful voice gave it new depth and meaning. We sat there silently and then Jim Barfield got up, went into the cage, and returned with his Bible opened.

"Read the whole thing, Hal," he said, handing Heep the Bible. Since that day I have heard many moving and beautiful sermons; I have heard Dean Gordon give memorable and thought-provoking sermons surrounded by the awesome stone beauty of the Princeton University Chapel; I have heard the clarity, the simplicity, and the great eloquence of a sermon by Bishop James Pike, but nothing has stirred me as did that simple rendition of the Song of Solomon by Hal Heep that Sunday morning so long ago. Perhaps it was the incongruity of the surroundings, or it may have been an awareness of who my fellow parishoners were; whatever the reason, that moment in my life is unforgettable.

We were an odd and disparate lot in that cage, and about the only factor we shared among us was that we all represented an appalling waste of human life. But to my mind the greatest waste of all was Tom Coughlin. Tom was one of the most perverse, maddening, likable cutthroats I have ever encountered—and this is a broad canvas. He was fantastically handsome in a rugged, masculine way . . . tall with broad powerful shoulders and narrow hips, and it was obvious women had spoiled him all his life. He had a great charm about him, and I think the secret of this charm lay in the genuine interest he took in other people. Even the warped-minded Boss Bray seemed fascinated by him.

On numerous occasions I had seen him look at Bray with a wide grin splitting his sun-blackened face and say, "Boss, you're so goddam mean and cantankerous, I almost love you. But don't ever turn your back on me . . . or I'll kill you."

Because of that flashing, even-toothed, white grin, Bray thought this was just a little joke the man was enjoying. Had he ever been close enough to Tom to see into the depths of those strange, almost-white eyes, he would have realized Tom was not joking. But taking it in jest, Bray would titter and come back with his unvarying rejoinder, "Nope, Tom . . . I'm gonna git you fust."

He was serving a life sentence for a murder that had grown out of a bank robbery, and his chance of ever being paroled or pardoned was about as slim as mine . . . only he had a previous record to nail his door shut a little more tightly. Loudly and boldly he would frequently state his credo: someday he would make good his escape and cut a swath across the entire South, and when "The Law" finally cornered him he would go down in a blaze of glory and take as many of "them" with him as he could. In my day I've heard of some wild and brainless ambitions, but this was the most bizarre one ever. It was especially puzzling coming from Tom, whom I had always considered a reasonably intelligent man; I knew he had graduated from high school, had served a four-year hitch in the navy, and had been all over the world. Tom doubtless considered his case hopeless, and rather than die in prison, a stir crazy, burned out old man, he had hit on this scheme of ending his days in a blaze of gunfire.

But despite this insane streak in him, Tom was always amusing and cheerful, and while he was slow in offering his friendship, once offered it became a sacred thing with him. Certainly Tom's presence on that gang made my life a little more bearable during the time he was there.

By now Travis was slowly slipping deeper and deeper into the depths of his own little private world. He rarely spoke these days, and when we were not working he would sit silently by himself, staring off into the middle distance with unseeing eyes. He seemed to be engulfed in a great sadness. And Boss Bray, who was himself growing madder by the minute, did not help matters by constantly nagging and picking at Travis. Every intuitive antenna in my being made me feel certain that things were building up to a climax; it was like watching the slow, relentless, inexorable folding of events in a Greek tragedy, and even the hands of the gods seemed powerless to stay it.

And then it happened.

On this particular work site the trusty mule skinners would leave with the teams and the wagons an hour and a half before we quit for the day. We would be picked up later by a civilian employee in an old chain-driven Mack Bulldog truck. The mule skinners would have to leave that much earlier in order to get to the camp, rub down the mules, and feed and water them before dark. And Grady would leave with them, for one of his duties was getting the mess shack set up for the evening meal. Later, having been strung onto the squad chain, we would climb onto the truck and be driven into the camp with Boss Bray, Brewer, and Charlie following behind in Bray's model T Ford touring car. But for this hour and a half there would be no trusties around, and Bray and the two guards would be alone with the gang.

It was the Kid who set this whole cauldron of hell boiling over. Somehow he had got his shackles loose—Bub had probably got him a piece of hacksaw blade—and he had refastened them with a piece of light string so that a simple jerk on them would cause them to fall off. Kicking off the shackles, he suddenly broke and ran for the nearby woods. He was traveling with the speed of a startled antelope, and in just a few more strides he would have made the safety of the thick woods. Brewer got off one round from his pump gun, but he fired too quickly and missed, and with that one round his gun jammed. Charlie, down at the far end of the cut, held his fire, realizing the Kid was out of range for an effective shot from his own pump gun. Bray quickly saw what was happening and, drawing Apollyon from its shoulder holster, leveled down on the fleeing figure of the Kid. Bray was an expert marksman with that handgun, and with his left hand behind his back he slowly, unhurriedly drew a bead on the Kid. The first shot got the Kid in the middle of the back right between the shoulder blades, and from the way he went down I knew he would not get up—ever. Unbelievably Bray was getting set to fire another shot into that sprawled figure when, in a whirring flash of motion, like a leaping tiger, Travis was on him. In the ensuing scuffle the gun was knocked from Bray's hand. Travis had him by the throat, and nothing could break the hold of those powerful hands. Brewer was still trying to clear his jammed gun, and Charlie was dancing around with his gun to his shoulder, trying to get off a shot at Travis, which, of course, he could not do without hitting Bray. Then Tom got into the act; in one leap he had the fallen revolver in his hand and, using the struggling figure of Bray as a shield, roared at Charlie, "Drop it, Charlie, drop it . . . and quick! Butt first . . . down the bank!"

The muzzle of that thirty-two-twenty must have looked as big around as a stove pipe to Charlie, for without hesitating he reversed the pump gun and slid it down the bank of the cut. In what I considered a towering act of idiocy a new man who had only been on the gang a few days now entered into all of this; I knew this new man had only a two-year sentence to serve, and I couldn't understand his point in becoming involved in all this big trouble. But scooping up Charlie's gun, he made the latter slide down from the bank and, prodding him along with the shotgun, marched him up to where Tom, having made Brewer drop his jammed gun, was forcing Brewer to also climb down from the bank. Bray was now down on his knees. His round little black felt hat had been knocked off his head, and that white bald head, the whiteness accentuated by the tan of his face, looked obscenely naked. True to his character, he was babbling incoherently but obviously pleading with Travis for his life. His little pig eyes kept rolling back into his head, and he was one of the most sickening sights I have ever had to look at. Never before or since have I seen a human being display such naked terror.

But there was ample reason for this terror, for Travis had taken the revolver from Tom and was standing looking down at him. Gone now from Travis was all the fog and vagueness with which he had been enveloped in the recent past; he was now a determined man who knew exactly what he was going to do. His lips were pulled back from his teeth in what could have been a snarl or a grin, but there was no grin in his eyes, and if Bray was even capable of seeing, he must have read his own death verdict in those eyes.

Tom had now picked up Brewer's pump gun and had cleared the jam. He was standing with it pointing at the two guards while actually watching Bray. That big, white grin of his was spread all over his face, as if this wild man was enjoying it all.

But Travis was something else: his lips were pulled back in the snarl of a ferocious beast which has escaped its cage and which now has its keeper at its mercy, the very keeper who has tormented it for years. There was no doubt in my mind that Bray was a dead man.

"I been waitin' for this a long time, ya bastard!" he snarled at Bray, and then his voice rose uncontrollably in an insane scream of rage. "AH, SO GODDAM LONG! . . . I oughta make ya die slow . . . DIE HARD! . . . but I ain't got the time!"

The revolver roared and jumped in his hand, and a black hole appeared in the center of Bray's forehead. All expression drained from his face, and with his eyes rolling up into his head, he pitched forward, twitched once, and lay sprawled in the deep dust with his arms outstretched. The back of that white, bald head was a sickening sight to see, and the black blood oozed out mixed with brains and ran down into the red dust.

"Now, you two bastards are next!" he screamed at Brewer and Charlie as he whirled on them with the gun leveled. Brewer was clearly in a state of shock, just standing there with his mouth hanging open and looking ashen under his tan. I am sure that I got a sense of satisfaction when I realized that my earlier estimation of Charlie had been correct; certainly my respect for him went up many notches when I saw him now—he was just standing there with his hands on his hips, looking back at Travis with a level stare. This man had much more to lose than the other two; he had a wife and two children, and certainly on his salary he could not have afforded much, if any, insurance for them. And from experience he knew that it was precious little either the county or the state would do for his dependents. But despite this, if he was to die, he would die as a man should, with dignity.

"NO! TRAVIS! NO!" I heard myself shout. "Those two haven't done anything to you . . . to us!"

And then Nobie, God bless him, helped me get some reason across to this crazed prisoner. "Let 'em alone, Travis! . . . and you're wasting valuable time. Get the hell out of here!"

The new man, the one who had picked up Charlie's shotgun, now dropped the gun and, moving away from Tom and Travis, came over and stood with the rest of us. "I don't want no part of no murder rap!" I guess the sight of Bray had brought him to his senses. I could not understand why he had wanted to get into this in the first place; it's all relative probably, but two years seemed to me like a sentence I could have made standing on my head.

Tom, by now realizing that they were wasting time, that every minute now could be worth hours later on, calmly started giving Travis orders. "Travis, get the keys to his car out of Bray's pocket while I make Charlie and Brewer take their clothes off. Get moving!"

Charlie had on a pair of underdrawers, but old Brewer, his spindly shanks exposed and his scrotum hanging halfway down to his knees, somehow looked even more naked than any naked man I had ever seen. But Tom now had two pairs of denim overalls and two blue hickory shirts. Turning to me, he said, "George, in the back of Bray's car is a small anvil, a hammer, and a chisel. Go get 'em, will ya? And, oh, yeah . . . somewhere in that car are those damned handcuffs of his . . . bring them too."

I knew about those tools in Bray's car. They were there in case a convict broke his leg and the shackles had to be removed quickly. I also knew about those "damned" handcuffs that Bray would use on occasion in one of his sadistic little schemes. At first it was with some hesitancy that I started on this errand, for with Brewer and Charlie as witnesses I knew that I could be charged with accessory-after-the-fact for even this amount of help, but then I suddenly remembered who I was, and chuckling to myself, I hurried off to Bray's car. With two life sentences hanging over me I did not see much else that society could throw my way. A death sentence? I didn't have much to lose.

When I returned, Tom snapped one end of one pair of the handcuffs around Brewer's right wrist and the other end around Charlie's left and then turned the two men around. Tom took the revolver from Travis, handed him the pump gun, and marched the two guards back up on the bank, where he handcuffed them around a tree with the other pair of cuffs. As Brewer turned around, I noticed that in his terror his sphincter muscles had turned loose and that his whole backside was covered with his own excrement.

Sliding back down into the cut and slipping the revolver into his waistband, Tom soon knocked the shackles off Travis's ankles, and then with a few blows of the hammer and chisel he freed his own legs. Then they both donned the overalls and blue shirts, and Tom, standing there with that flashing grin, looked over toward us. "Any of you guys want to knock your chains off and join us . . . be my guest."

Naturally he had no takers, for there was not a man on that gang who did not realize that these two would be hunted to the ends of the earth, and that they would never be taken alive; they had committed the one unforgivable crime in the eyes of any law officer . . . the killing of a policeman or prison guard.

"No—thank—you," I said with emphasis. "But, Tom . . . you're going to need this." And pulling out my Prince Albert can "safe," I fished out a tightly rolled ten-dollar bill I had been hoarding and pushed it into Tom's free hand. To a man that gang followed suit, and in a minute the two had close to a hundred dollars in their initial kitty.

"Thank you, guys, thank you," Tom said, bowing from the waist to the whole gang. "We'll think of you often!"

Then coming over to Nobie and me, he said quietly, the grin gone now, "Seriously, I wish you two were going with us . . . you're two guys I'd like to die with."

Nobie and I just grinned at him, but I think we did mumble something about "Good luck!"

With this they both ran to Bray's car and, cranking it up, whirled it around. With Tom driving, they tore down the road with the hand throttle all the way down, heading for freedom . . . but more likely to the jaws of hell.

When they were gone I suddenly realized that in all the excitement I had not seen Bub Fletcher. Looking over to where the Kid's body had fallen, I saw the great bearlike figure sitting on the ground, cradling the Kid's lifeless body in his arms, tears streaming down his face, moaning softly, and brushing the Kid's hair back from his forehead.

5.

A week later we heard that Tom and Travis been stopped at a police roadblock in Louisiana, that they had been recognized and riddled with bullets before the stolen car they were in had come to a full halt. Tom didn't get his chance to take any of "them" with him.

On the following Sunday Heep, Nobie, and I were sitting on our dynamite box "rocking chairs" in front of the cage and were discussing the human waste that was represented in the short life of Tom Coughlin.

"Well . . . rob a man of hope . . ." Heep said quietly. "But, y'know, to my mind the death of the Kid is an even bigger human waste. Right out of a reformatory into a chain gang . . . and then on top of that, a homosexual experience. My God . . . what chance would that boy ever have had in life—even if Bray hadn't murdered him?"

Silently I fell to thinking of the many things I had already learned in prison, things that the Kid too would have learned had he lived. From the elite of the prison society, the petermen, any eager young mind would learn the fine art of blowing a safe. He would learn how to render the nitroglycerin from stolen dynamite and then how to use soft soap to make troughs around the cracks in the door of the safe and how to trickle—"Gently, damn it!"—this soup into the troughs. He would learn how to attach the dynamite cap and the fuse and then to cover the whole assemblage with rugs and carpets to best muffle the blast . . .

From others of the elite corps, the bank robbers, he would learn that only punks rob filling stations and grocery stores—"Go where the money's at . . . the banks. You ain't going to get in any more trouble . . . and the pay-off's bigger."

If he had any education and was smart, he would learn from the con men, first the "short" con men, who live by their wits and who know endless tricks for bilking honest people out of a few dollars; but if he was really smart and could put on a good front, he could easily learn the imaginative tricks of the "long" con artists. Very few of this brotherhood ever wound up in prison, for their stock in trade consisted of appealing to the wide streak of larceny inherent in us all. Which one of us, ever, would be willing to go into open court and testify before a judge and a jury that he had been hoodwinked out of a considerable sum of money by a smooth-talking crook who had persuaded him he could turn a fast, dishonest dollar?

The Kid would undoubtedly have met my friend Jerry Klein, who was wrapping up a four-year sentence for selling eight black boxes for five thousand dollars apiece. Of course these were extraordinary boxes, Rube Goldberg boxes, three feet long by eighteen inches square with handles and cranks and adjusting valves on them and two receptacles on top for holding india ink. In one end was a slot for the insertion of the proper size of blank paper—"It's most important you

use only a very high quality, heavy rag content paper . . ."
—and in the other end another slot out of which would appear brand-new, crisp five-dollar bills when the crank was
turned.

The poor state's attorney. Where would he ever find a
victim who would come into court and testify he had been
bilked out of $5,000 for an utterly worthless "counterfeiting"
machine? In desperation John Boykin, the prosecutor, had
allowed Jerry to plead guilty and had acceded to a four-year
sentence, provided Jerry leave the state of Georgia forever
on his release. Forty thousand dollars for four years seemed
a bargain to my friend Jerry.

Jerry had conceived his brilliant scheme while serving
time in the Montana State Prison at Deer Lodge. Another
friend of mine who had not wasted his time in prison was
Clinton Samuel Carnes. At this time Clinton was in his mid-
fifties—tall, spare, distinguished-looking—and serving seven
years for embezzlement. Twenty years previously he had
been sentenced to three years in a federal prison for a
crime of which he claimed to be innocent; he vowed he
would make society pay for this injustice, and on his release
he changed his name, moved to Atlanta, and became a respected businessman. He also became a pillar in the Baptist
church, and because he was a wizard with figures, he was soon
appointed treasurer of the Baptist Home Mission Board.
Here, if ever, was an example of what Nikita Khrushchev, at a
later date, was to call "sending the pigs to mind the turnips."
Very shortly even the Baptists began to realize something was
wrong, and the auditing firm of Ernst & Ernst was called in
to go over the books. It is doubtful if this old firm had ever
before run into such a tangled web of juggled figures, but
when the audit was finished it was estimated that $953,000
was missing. Clinton Samuel Carnes just grinned like a
Cheshire cat and again . . . poor John Boykin. Because
even he couldn't quite figure out what had happened, he was
unable to get across to a jury the full dollar magnitude of

the crime that had been committed, and the jury, as confused as everyone else, settled for a sentence of seven years. With time off for good behavior he would serve five years, and he in his turn considered five years for a million dollars a bargain.

It is doubtful whether the Kid would have got to know Clinton Carnes, for Clinton had been transferred to the state prison farm, where he was a full trusty, living in a room of his own behind the office. Even the guards called him "Mr. Carnes," for in this dollar-oriented society of ours a million dollars is to be respected, no matter what its source.

Had the Kid lived, he would have learned many other things during his two years in prison, learned them at society's expense, and when he got out and started putting this knowledge to practice and got into more trouble, society would call for harsher laws, for speedier justice, and for "lawanorder."

Probably the Kid—and society too, for that matter—would never have appreciated the truth in the words of G. K. Chesterton: "It's not that they can't see the solution . . . they can't see the problem."

However, as the result of that grisly afternoon a series of changes began to take place in my life as a convict. There was, of course, a grand jury investigation, and ten of us were taken before this grand jury to testify as to what had happened that afternoon. I had the impression the county solicitor general, after he got his two indictments for murder, would have quietly closed the matter and considered the follow-up to be police business. However, the foreman of the jury was a man with considerable social consciousness, and he had no intention of letting this become a mere swept-under-the-carpet, routine matter. Besides being a medical doctor, he was a man of rare intelligence who possessed some state-wide political influence.

Each of us was questioned separately about the events that precipitated this investigation, and then the doctor took over the questioning. Comparing experiences later with the others, it became apparent that he started his questioning with the same statement to each of us.

"George, I want the truth about conditions in that camp out there" were his opening words to me. "I want you to hold nothing back from me and the other members of this jury. For this truth on your part I'll guarantee that no reprisals will be taken against you by any prison official. Of course, you will have to take on face value my promise that this will be so. Obviously you could not write me should any reprisals take place. But I give you my word that from time to time I will visit you, no matter where you are, to make sure my end of this bargain is being upheld. Now, let's begin . . ."

He was an elderly man with a suntanned, rugged, beat-up face like an old barn door, and somehow one felt instinctively he could be trusted. Added to this was the strange sense of freedom we all felt now that Boss Bray was dead. Because of these two factors we all opened up and told the truth and under the doctor's questioning gave our suggestions for reforms we thought were needed. Apparently we all made sense and none of us made any absurd claims or suggestions, for each one of us was kept in the jury room for about the same length of time. For my part I pointed out the evil of a system that would mix together in one camp and on the same work gangs older, hardened men serving up to life for murder and young boys of sixteen or seventeen serving three months for hoboing on freight trains. We all told of the illegal use of the lash. For a moment I started to speak of hopelessness, the frustration that lies at the root of crime, dope addiction, and most alcoholism. Then I remembered to whom I was speaking—a cross-section of white, middle-class, Christian Americans—and I knew they wouldn't understand. Nor would they—other than the doctor—much care. So, I spoke instead of something they would understand —stale piss—and I tried to make that jury smell those urine-soaked wooden tubs which were in each cage. Then I was asked about homosexuality in the camp and what remedies I would suggest. What "remedies" are there? The doctor and the jurymen all agreed that my suggestion of castrating the lot of us was rather drastic, but under the system of mixing older men with young boys the problem of homosexuality was inevitable. I don't remember it now, but all of us must have talked about the food, for I've never seen a convict who didn't gripe about prison food. It's a privilege, a right, he picks up in court along with his sentence.

By three o'clock that afternoon the questioning was over, and the doctor had all of us brought back into the jury room together. He thanked us for our help, told us that each story had corroborated the others, and reiterated his promise of protection against reprisals. Then, turning to the county solicitor, and in front of all of us, he said with authority in his voice, "Mr. Ellis, I want these men taken by deputy sheriffs —accompanied by men from your office—back out to the camp. They are to be allowed to gather up what belongings they possess and then they are to be returned here to the county jail. I want them held here until I can reach Governor Russell by phone and their future assignments are decided on."

The reach of this man's political power may be gauged by the solicitor general's reply, "Very good, Dr. Hemple."

Then, turning back to us, he said one final thing. "This mess has made headlines all over the South. I'm going to suggest—I'm going to ask—that you not speak to the press. For your own sakes I think it best. Just tell them, 'No Comment.' I'll give out a statement to the newspapers later. And, boys . . . good luck!"

Dr. Hemple must have reached the governor by phone that afternoon, for by midafternoon of the following day the three members of the Georgia State Prison Commission came to see us in the jail. After questioning us for some minutes about the case, Judge Dunaway, a large, corpulent man who was the chairman, told us, "The governor has suggested that you ten men be sent to Fulton County. As soon as Fulton can arrange the transfer you'll be moved up there."

Fulton County. I felt as though I were going home. Besides being the county surrounding Atlanta, it had the reputation of having the most modern and humane prison system in the state of Georgia. There were six separate work camps in addition to a smaller camp, the River Camp, for disabled, sick, and aged prisoners. Each camp had wooden barracks with flush toilets and hot and cold showers; there was a large headquarters camp, Bellwood, where there was a fully equipped fourteen-bed hospital that served the whole system. Each camp had its own garden, which meant fresh vegetables in the summer, and there was a small store in each from which a few luxuries could be purchased. But above all, no matter to which of the camps I would be assigned, it would be only a short drive on visiting days for the three people I loved. I had heard much about the camps in Fulton County from other convicts, for it was the mecca, the Arcadia, for any convict in the whole Georgia penal setup. A few years previously I would never have thought that I would look forward to going to any prison, but I suppose all values are dependent on their framework.

Two days later, around noon, the transfer guards from Fulton County arrived; there were two of them in two new Model A Ford station wagons with the Fulton County seal painted on the sides; they were accompanied by three blue-uniformed Fulton County policemen in a black Buick sedan. While the two transfer men who drove the station wagons were unarmed, the policemen were heavily armed, and as we were led out of the jail to the waiting cars, I noticed there were several pump guns and lever-action rifles in the back of the Buick which would follow along closely on the drive to Atlanta. As we were still wearing our chains and shackles, it was obvious there would be no escaping on this trip.

It was a good thing they had brought station wagons, for

each of us had a dynamite box with a makeshift lid on it in which we kept our belongings—our "needments," as Heep called them—and in addition to these Heep and I had our stack of books. But the others helped us with these, and we set out on the long drive wedged in by our possessions.

We arrived late that night in Atlanta, and the small convoy wove through the streets of Atlanta, down Prior Street to Marietta and then down Decatur to Butler Street. I saw all the lights and the store fronts and the busy people going about their night business, and I had the odd sensation that I had returned to civilization after a nightmare trip to some Never-Never Land. Boss Bray and those cages and those urine tubs and Travis and that afternoon of tempestuous violence all seemed far away and a long time ago, and I felt sure that none of these people, laughing and lining up under movie marquees, or walking in couples down the streets, or going into restaurants, would even know what I was talking about if I could stop and get out and tell them. I also had the feeling they wouldn't care.

Just after passing through the maze of street intersections that was Five Points, we were held up momentarily by traffic. Most of the stores were still open, for this was 1932 and the shop keepers were battling for every penny they could get. We stopped opposite a music store, and a loud-speaker was blaring a hit tune of the day. A woman's plaintive voice was singing, "Look down, look down . . . that lonesome road, before you travel on . . ."

I wondered on that night how long this lonesome road I was traveling would continue and over what far-distant horizon it would stretch.

We were kept that night in the old Fulton County Tower, the jail in which I had spent many agonizing months of my life. During that time I had become friendly with the old turnkeys, and now the ones who were still on duty came to our cell to see me. It seemed almost like some crazy sort of reunion. After a warm late supper we got to shave and enjoyed a shower under hot water, and when I lay down on a bunk in that cell, life actually had some rosy tints around the edges.

The next morning at six o'clock the same small convoy, manned by the same personnel, picked us up, and we drove out the Bankhead Highway to Bellwood, the receiving and headquarters camp. We had been joined by two Negroes and a white boy who had just been sentenced and who were starting their terms on this day. Apparently the Negroes were both old hands at this business, for the transfer guards knew them and joked with them all during the half-hour drive.

"Damn, Cliff," one of them said to a large, one-eyed Negro. "I knowed dang well you'd be back . . . but, man, your bunk ain't even cold yet. What happened this time?"

"Well, ya see, Mistuh Elmer . . . I was standin' there mindin' my own business . . . an' this heah bright-skin boy . . . well, he jist kinda run into the knife I jist happen to be holdin' in my hand an' . . ."

"You mean to tell me Judge Wood didn't believe you! Cliff, you been framed again."

"Ah knows it, Mistuh Elmer . . . Ah cain't git justice in that man's court."

"Poor ol' Cliff . . . wal, your job's waitin' for ya in the kitchen."

Both the Negroes were old-timers, but this was the first trip for the white boy. The fright on his face was almost painful to behold, and it was obvious he had never been in a reformatory and was therefore not prepared for this experience. But he would get over this fright, he would become inured to prison life, and he would then start his education as a criminal. I offered up a silent prayer that he and I would be sent to separate camps; I'd already seen enough young boys being coached and schooled in cynicism and savagery to sour my guts for the rest of my life. I hoped to be spared this one.

6.

The sprawling acres that comprised Bellwood Camp were enclosed in miles of barbed-wire fence. After being admitted through a large double-hung gate we were driven for a quarter of a mile down a plane-tree-lined road. On either side were rows of parked road machinery, machine shops, and warehouses. I had always known that Fulton County, being the center of the industrial complex that surrounded Atlanta, was one of the richest counties in the entire South; but for the first time I began to realize that the county's Public Works Department was big business, and the chain gang system was an integral part of it. The county at that time used the labor of almost two thousand convicts, roughly half of whom were felons convicted of major crimes in the state courts, the others being short-termers convicted of misdemeanors in the county courts. In addition to this work force the Public Works Department also employed one thousand civilians who served as guards, truck drivers, and mule skinners, and in other capacities for which convict labor could not be used.

One of the first things I noticed at Bellwood was the difference in the thinking of the warden, the deputy wardens, the foremen, and the guards as compared to the official thinking to which I had grown accustomed. These men were better paid and for the most part better educated than had been the officials in the backwoods gangs. Also they were backed up by the wealth and the power of Fulton County. They did not have to be afraid of us, therefore they did not have to be cruel. In addition, the self-righteous attitude that they were official administrators of punishment never entered their heads; we, the convicts, were co-workers on a job that had to be done—the building and the maintenance of the highways of Fulton County.

After the records clerk—and his trusty assistant—had properly inducted us into the penal population of this county, we were given hot showers, issued new striped clothing that fit us, led over to a clean mess hall that smelled of pine disinfectant, and given a good breakfast. There were hot white-flour biscuits instead of the usual slabs of half-cooked corn pone.

Only one of the guards had accompanied us from the office over to the mess hall. I was eating at one end of the bare, scrubbed pine table. Across from me was a vacant place on the bench, and now this guard sat down and looked across at me.

"So you're Harsh," he said, rather than asked.

From my experience with prison guards I was a bit chary of what might be coming. "Yes sir," I said continuing to eat.

"Man, I sure remember readin' about you. Them newspapers give you a fit, didn't they?"

"Yessir . . . I got my share of unwanted publicity."

"Yeah . . . as I remember that jury of yourn only stayed out fifteen minutes. It ain't no wonder. For months before the trial them newspapers tried you, convicted you, and burned you in the electric chair there every day."

"I guess I'm lucky to be here."

"That's one way of lookin' at it, I reckon." I began to relax now, for apparently this man was just trying to be friendly. He was perhaps in his mid-forties and seemed calm and sure of himself in a quiet way. He was deeply tanned, and I noticed the crow's-feet at the corners of his eyes. These could have come from constant squinting in the sun, but I got the impression that good-humored laughter had put a lot of them there.

"Wal, you ain't got nothin' to worry about . . . here in Fulton County we ain't tryin' to prove nothin'."

After we finished eating, the guard told us we could smoke here in the mess hall, that we would have a short wait until the county physician arrived to give us a quick physical examination, and that then we would be sent out to the various side camps to which we had been assigned. Nobie and Heep were sitting on either side of me.

"You three are lucky," he said looking over at us after consulting a sheaf of papers he had attached to a clipboard. "Mr. Bub Clarke—he's the chief warden—looked over your records an' he's sendin' y'all up to North Camp. That's up above Buckhead."

My luck was holding. Heep, Nobie, and I would stay together.

"Claud Mills . . . he's the deputy warden in charge up there, the guard continued. "He's tough as a ruttin' boar hog . . . but he's fair. I know. I worked up there at North Camp for five years. He'll give you long-timers a break—if you'll let him. But don't never cross him up. He's a deacon in the Baptist church . . . but he sure in hell don't hold none with this turnin' of the other cheek business. His son Carl, he's only twenty-seven years old, but he's foreman of the gang that's got most of the lifers and long-termers. He's just like his pappy . . . tough as hell, but fair. He'll give y'all a break."

At this point a Negro trusty in gray pants stuck his head in the door. "Mistuh Morgan . . . the Doc's heah."

"C'mon, y'all," the guard said, getting to his feet. "Over to the hospital."

The ten of us transferred men and the three newly committed ones who had joined us this morning were marched over to the hospital, a large one-story white frame building set off by itself. The wide nail-studded door was standing open, and we were told to line up along one wall of an examination room. Seated at a table in the back of the room was a tall, spare man with a clipped mustache and wearing horn-rimmed glasses. Standing next to him was a Negro trusty in gray trousers and a starched white jacket. On the table in front of the doctor was a stethoscope, a sphygmomanometer, and a small pile of filing cards. Picking up one of these cards, he called out, "Harsh."

Going over to the table, I stood in front of it and waited while he read what had been typed on the card he was holding. Then he motioned to the chair beside the table, and I sat down.

"M-m . . . so, you're Harsh. I certainly read a lot about you a couple of years ago. I guess you're damn' glad to get off those front pages." As he said this he looked up and grinned at me. "My name's McDonald . . . Paul McDonald. I'm supposed to be a doctor . . . although there're times when I have my doubts about that. Anyway . . . anything the matter with you?"

"No, sir, not that I know of. I certainly feel healthy."

"You sure look it. Stand up, take your shirt off, and let me listen to you."

After the superficial examination he told me to be seated again. "I tell this to all you lifers," he began quietly so that only I and the Negro trusty could hear him. "There'll be times out there when you want a day of rest . . . and you'll need that occasionally. Every once in a while you'll need just a quiet day in bed when you'll not be surrounded by the constant babble of voices. It sounds silly, I know, but life is a long time, and I'm always ready to help you lifers. Occasionally, when you want that day of rest, report sick and stay in bed. And when I get out there on my rounds, tell me what you're doing . . . don't try to shit me and have me waste time looking for symptoms. I'll give you some sugar pills, write something in Latin on your records, and we'll be the only two who know about it . . . you, me, and the rest of you lifers. But don't overdo it."

"I won't, Doctor. And thank you very much, sir."

7.

After a few months in the North Camp Heep,
Nobie, and I were made trusties. Claud Mills,
assessing our records and deciding that the three of us
wanted our freedom only through legal channels, ordered
our chains and shackles cut off and had gray cotton trousers
and shirts issued to us. Again I am speaking of frameworks:
one of the great moments of my life will remain that night
the shackles were removed from my ankles.

Lord Byron tells us that The Prisoner of Chillon lost his
chains "with a sigh." Somehow I doubt this, but should it
prove to be true I would be inclined to believe, from my
experience, that Byron's Prisoner was suffering from an advanced stage of stir-craziness. I lost my chains with a glad cry
—not vocally, but in my soul. When the last hammer stroke
on the chisel bit through the rivets, and the shackles and
chains fell from my legs and rattled on the wooden floor, my
spirit soared upward like a meadowlark that someone had

failed to cage. I suppose it sounds strange to say that one could feel "free" while still in prison. In the poetry of truth Nobie summed up the feeling of the three of us. "You guys know sumpin'?" He grinned at Heep and me. "For a long time I been wanting, on occasion, to kick one or the other of you in the ass. Look out . . . now I can do it!"

Our legs felt airy and light, and we knew then how Hermes must have felt in his winged sandals. But the habit of walking with a short, pigeon-toed stride had become ingrained, and it was some months before we again learned to walk with a normal gait.

From that night on, my life became more than a mere struggle for survival, a day-to-day grim routine of sweat-sodden toil. I began to hope that maybe my future life could have more meaning than the senseless giving of an eye for an eye.

Nobie became a general roustabout, a Jack-of-all-trades who would fill in for the other trusties when one of them was ill or injured, and he was available to perform those tasks which had to be carried out beyond the reach of the shotguns or which would keep him out of sight, often for hours on end. Freed from the mind-rotting routine, Nobie was now in a position to do his time and retain his sanity even should he be denied a parole or pardon.

Heep, because he could read and interpret the profiles and blueprints supplied by the county highway engineers, was made responsible for the grades and fills on the roads we were building; he too was now in a position to serve his full time if necessary.

The opening occurred and I was made the water boy for Carl Mills's gang of long-termers. There was nothing challenging about the job, but at least I was now able to help in small ways those who were unable to help themselves. The most rewarding aspect of the new job was that now, frequently, I could be alone with my thoughts, out of earshot and sight of other human beings, and could revel in the luxury of solitude. My new life wasn't the way I wanted to spend the rest of my days, but I knew now that I could . . . well, weather one day at a time without too much physical strain or spiritual frustration.

One of my duties was taking care of the pack of eight bloodhounds that accompanied Mr. Carl's squad of long-termers on every job to which it was assigned. One of the civilian mule skinners, a man by the name of Efe Dowell, would bring the pack with him in his wagon every morning, and it was my job to meet them, unload them, and lead them into the shade of the trees, where they would be kept chained during the day. I had to see that they had plenty of water and generally look after them during the day; at night (and early in the morning before we left for work) I had to give them their meal of scraps from the guards' table. From my earliest childhood there has always been a dog in my life, and during this period on the chain gang I especially enjoyed my friendship with that pack of bloodhounds.

Most people believe that a pack of bloodhounds, catching its prey on the ground, will rip the quarry into bloody ribbons. This is simply not so. When a pack overtakes its quarry it circles the fugitive, each dog wagging its tail and baying out its plea for the fugitive to, please, run some more and let's continue this great fun.

In fact there is a recorded instance in the annals of Georgia criminology wherein an escaped convict, knowing the characteristics of bloodhounds, tied up the whole pack with a rope leash after they had caught up with him and took this valuable pack to Chattanooga. There he sold the dogs for one hundred dollars, and with this money rode to freedom in style in a parlor car of the Southern Railroad.

Six months after we had been made trusties it became known that Heep was suffering from tuberculosis. For the past several months Nobie and I had been noticing the dry, persistent cough which he had developed. We had noticed that quietly, without saying anything about it, he had given up smoking, but the cough persisted and, if anything, had grown slightly worse. Also, while he had always been lean and wiry he now seemed to be losing weight, and this was weight he could ill afford in view of the long hours he worked. All of this was not anything sudden or dramatic; it had been taking place over an extended period and would probably have gone unnoticed had not all of us been living in such a close and intimate relationship. Recently Nobie had suggested to him, in an almost offhand manner, that he report in sick some morning and let the doctor listen to his cough; but Heep had brushed aside the idea and the matter was not mentioned again. But soon the cough became a racking, almost constant thing, and on occasion he would spit up the "brick dust" sputum of advanced tuberculosis. Carl Mills had a high regard for the man and was doing all he could to make life a little easier and more bearable for him. On numerous occasions he would make Heep take a day off and remain in camp for a day of rest. I found out that on two of these days he had gone in to meet Dr. McDonald to talk to him about Hal. Nobie and I too were becoming increasingly worried about our friend, and when we were alone we often discussed Heep. One night after Hal had seen the doctor, Nobie and I questioned him as to what the doctor had said. Apparently Dr. McDonald had laid it on the line to him, telling him that he could have him transferred either to the state farm at Milledgville or to the River Camp in the Fulton County system; however, he pointed out to Heep that conditions at the state farm were just short of deplorable and that, in his opinion, Heep would be better off where he was. Transferring him to the River Camp wouldn't improve anything either, for no more could be done for him there than could be done in his present surroundings. The doctor had gone into detail with Heep and had held nothing back from him: his one chance was to get to a sanatorium, where one lung at a time could be collapsed and immobilized to give the lung a chance to rest and heal itself. Short of this Heep's days were numbered.

We learned that on two occasions the doctor had gone personally to the State Prison Commissison with a plea for clemency, but those politicians were under such pressure from the relatives of prisoners with money and from high-powered lawyers that the case of Heep, a penniless unknown, was an easy one for them to simply sweep under the carpet. As Heep told us this he made a brave attempt to be cheer-ful and offhand, but his act did not come off to me. I could see that he was gripped by the great sadness that comes over a man when he is finally faced with inevitable death.

Several days later I had a chance to talk to Heep alone, and I brought up the question as to what he could do should he gain his freedom.

"I've got a sister and brother-in-law in Boston—which is actually my home—not New York—and the three of us have always been very close. They both have good jobs and, even in these depressed times, they're financially secure. They'd help me. Also—strange as it seems—the archbishop up there is a friend of mine . . . he'd help me. But why? What's on your mind?"

"Escape."

"Oh, come on, George . . . that's hopeless."

"Nope. It can be done . . . and God damn it, man, it's your only chance!"

"But . . . you mean from the job?"

"Sure."

"But the dogs . . ."

"I can take care of the dogs. You'll have a rough time for three days . . . but we can do it. Are you game to try?"

For the past week the powder monkeys—semitrusties whose job it was to drill by hand the blasting holes up on the face of the cut—had been drilling, and I knew that on Friday morning Carl Mills planned to have the holes filled with blasting powder so he could set off these charges on Friday afternoon. Once the blast had been set off and as soon as the smoke had cleared Mr. Carl, Nobie, and I would have to return to the site to make sure that all the holes had blown and that there was neither raw powder nor unexploded dynamite lying around before the squad would be returned to work. All of this would take at least two hours—with Nobie and me dragging our feet it might even take a little longer—and during this time Heep would be alone and unsupervised down on the fill. He would have at least a two-hour start before he would be missed; but even after two hours the hounds, by circling the fill base, could still pick up his trail, and because of the ground they could cover they would soon catch up to him if he were still afoot. No doubt those hounds were going to be a problem; and I hated to think of my pets baying at the heels of my friend Hal Heep.

At two o'clock that Friday afternoon I took a bucket of water down to the fill to give Heep a drink. Setting the bucket down, I reached into my pocket and handed Heep a roll of small bills bound with a rubber band: the roll contained one hundred dollars—all that Nobie and I could scrape together. But back in those days when a dollar was worth one hundred cents the amount would be adequate for the purpose.

"Hal, we haven't got any time to waste," I said, feeling the sense of urgency growing within me. "So, don't say anything—just listen. You know that spring where I get the water? . . . well, down below it is the creek. Follow that creek north for about a mile and on your left you'll come to a huge old willow on the creek bank. Under those drooping branches is a perfect shelter . . . it's almost like a cave in there. Under there you'll find a pair of overalls and a blue shirt. And tied up to the trunk of the tree is a brown paper bag with some cheese sandwiches and chocolate bars in it. You're going to have to live on that for three days. You can drink the creek water—it won't kill you. BUT STAY

UNDER THAT TREE FOR THREE DAYS! Then, on the fourth night come out and keep following that creek north. About ten miles on up the creek you'll come to a railroad. Stay in the woods as much as possible but follow that railroad, and eventually you'll get to Rome, Georgia. From Rome you can get a bus to Chattanooga, and from there you can get a train to New York. Now, repeat all that to me . . . let's make sure you got it."

Almost word for word he quoted the directions back to me, and then he started to say something else—to thank me.

"Hold it," I interrupted. "When you get that TB arrested and get your collar on backwards again—burn a candle for me . . . or whatever the hell you people do."

I don't think he trusted himself to look at me—and I'm just as glad he didn't. When he turned his back to me I heard him mutter, as though talking to himself, "Merciful God . . ."

With Nobie's help I was able to drag out the blasting time longer than usual, and it was almost three hours before the first dirt-laden wagon with its civilian mule skinner arrived at the fill. Immediately the alarm went up and the hue and cry was on; escapes were not commonplace, but they did occur from time to time, and the procedures of the chase followed a routine pattern: Carl Mills naturally directed the operation, and his first act was to send one of the mule skinners with the youngest and fastest team to the nearest farmhouse that had a telephone to notify the county police and the camp. Efe Dowell, the skinner who handled the dogs, and three other civilian employees armed with revolvers came for the pack which I had ready and, with the dogs still leashed, began circling the fill to pick up Heep's scent. The first outside help to arrive was Claud Mills, whose car was followed by two other vehicles, bearing all the available off-duty guards. Next there arrived three county police cars with Police Lieutenant Carroll in the lead car. After Carl gave them a description of Heep, Carroll pulled out a map of the area and assigned the waiting cars, both police and guards, to the roads they were to patrol. They were to range as far north as Roswell and south to Buckhead, and from time to time they were to stop, shut off their motors, and listen for the baying of the hounds, which would give them a converging point. The radios in the police cars were crackling, and the state-wide search was being organized.

Unnoticed I slipped down to the fill, and standing there, I watched Efe Dowell and the three other civilians with the hounds, which slowly circled the base of the fill, sniffing for the scent. Suddenly Old Row, the patriarch of the pack and the veteran of many a chase, threw back his old graying head and let forth with his bugle—he had the scent. And then the whole pack let loose with their yammering and yowling, and with the dogs' tails wagging and their noses to the ground, the chase was on.

But suddenly something happened. The pack with Old Row in the lead had not gone more than ten yards when suddenly they stopped almost as though they had slammed on the brakes. As one dog the whole pack threw its collective head in the air and then, bobbing their noses to the ground, let out a loud and simultaneous "Ker–CHOO!" Shaking their heads, they tried the scent again, and within a few feet the communal "Ker–CHOO!" again echoed from the surrounding woods.

"Sorry, old buddies," I murmured to myself as I saw the pained and perplexed look come over the faces of my friends. "But you'll get over it."

"What the hell!" I heard Mr. Carl's voice shout. I had not noticed him come up on the fill beside me. "Efe! Range 'em out a hundred yards . . . circle and try to pick up the scent farther out!"

Rechaining the pack, Efe and the three skinners led the dogs further off, and after again circling for a few minutes they again had the scent—and the whole ludicrous, unbelievable thing happened again; only this time the king-sized

"Ker–CHOO!" was music to my ears. I was sure now that pack would never follow *this* scent.

Muttering a string of imaginative cuss words, Carl ran from the fill toward the lone police car that had been left behind as a radio-contact headquarters. I saw him talking and gesticulating to the policeman as the latter began speaking into the microphone. Standing there on the fill and watching as Efe tried once more to get that baffled pack back onto the scent, I cut a huge chew from a plug of Days' Work tobacco. I hoped chewing the oversize cud would hide the smug, self-satisfied grin on my face.

My plan had worked. And I was sure by now Heep was safely hidden under the drooping branches of the old willow; if he would just stay there for three days, with any luck at all, he had it made. A lesser man, under the circumstances, might find it hard to lie doggo for three days, but on this score I had no worry about Heep—if need be he could play a mental game of chess with himself for this period. And he could always sprinkle pepper on the cheese sandwiches—and chuckle to himself.

When I handed Heep the roll of bills I also handed him two Bull Durham tobacco sacks filled with pepper, and I showed him how to tie these to the backs of his ankles so that every step he took would be liberally dusted with pepper. At first I had some doubt about the plan . . . but now the doubt was removed. Pepper and hounds' noses have the same incompatibility as do water and oil.

Later that afternoon, after repeated attempts had failed to get the pack on the scent, I went up to visit them and take them some water. Stopping at the edge of the clearing and setting down the bucket, I stood for a moment with my hands on my hips looking at them. The great chew in my cheek was still helping to hide the expression on my face. The hounds, which had been lying down, got slowly to their feet, and all eight pairs of eyes were on me, watching me with some apprehension as though they feared what my reaction to their failure to perform might be. A couple of them tried a tentative wag of the tail, but I could sense the prevailing fear of disapprobation that gripped them. Li'l Lady, the puppy of the pack, was having a hard time forcing herself to face me at all. I knew it was cruel to prolong their suspense, so throwing back my head, I let go with a loud "Ker–CHOO!" and grinned at them. Suddenly they knew it was all right, that it had all been some sort of game, and that everything was as it should be. They all began talking at once and wagging their tails, and I was afraid Li'l Lady would choke herself on her leash before I could get to her and hug her.

The next morning during a moment when Carl Mills and I were alone he said, looking at me speculatively, "George, what d'you suppose happened to those hounds yesterday? I've never seen a pack act that way before."

"I dunno, Mr. Carl . . . maybe they ran into some kind of weed they're allergic to."

"Hm-m . . . like maybe a pepper plant. Oh, well . . . I guess that's as good an explanation as any."

Then, without any reason for doing so, he said, "Lieutenant Carroll told me that the police were going to patrol the roads of the entire area for the rest of the day, and then by nightfall, if they haven't turned up a trace of Heep, they're going to mark him on the records as 'Escaped' and get on with their other police work."

The deep sigh I heaved almost knocked the hat from his head. But I could have sworn I detected a slight sigh coming from him too.

8.

Although Carl Mills knew that in some way I had aided and abetted the escape of Hal Heep, both he and his father recommended me when a job for a full trusty opened up in the Bellwood Hospital.

At this time Surgeon General Parran of the United States Public Health Service, with the courage of a true physician, decided to break through the myths, pruderies, and ignorance surrounding syphilis and eradicate this inexcusable disease from the American scene. With the help of all the news media he started a campaign to educate the public. To begin with, syphilis was no longer to be referred to daintily as a "social disease" but was to be called openly by its dirty name. The myth that the disease could be contracted from door knobs and toilet seats was to be laughed into limbo, and the public was to be educated that the only means of contraction was through sexual intercourse. Not "scare stories," but true articles were to appear in the news media graphically depicting the woes, ravages, and miseries attendant on this disease unless medical help was obtained quickly. The newspapers and magazines of that period did a magnificent job, and lurking, ignorance-shielded syphilis was brought out into the open where all-out war could be waged against it.

The weapon to be used in this war was the chain of free Public Health Service clinics established across the entire country. It was a gigantic undertaking involving millions of dollars and many thousands of dedicated, tireless doctors, nurses, and social workers. The fact that this campaign of education and treatment succeeded as well as it did is a shining tribute to the zeal, determination, and organizational ability of one truly remarkable man—Dr. Thomas Parran, surgeon general of the United States in 1936.

Clinics were established in all the prisons of the country. In due course one of these was set up in the Fulton County, Georgia, penal system, and that is how I entered into the campaign. I was a very small cog in a vast machine, but because of my limited efforts of those days, I am better able to bear the memories of a largely regrettable life.

During the next five years of my life I was associated with, and gained the enduring friendship of, two outstanding men and one memorable woman.

Dr. Paul McDonald was one of those medical men who have disappeared from the modern scene—the general practitioner who has to be his own specialist. Also he was practicing medicine before the discovery of the many miracle drugs; his pharmacopoeia was a slim volume compared to the modern one, and he had to rely mainly on common sense and vast experience to effect his cures. Certainly medicine today is a more exact and precise science than it was in the days of Paul McDonald; but whether it is "better" is a moot point, for it has lost the humanity of the old general practitioner. By any yardstick Paul McDonald was a great man, and I treasure the memory of my five years' association and friendship with him.

Rudolph Hillyer was the Negro trusty in the starched white jacket who had been standing beside Dr. McDonald on the morning of my admission to the Fulton County chain gang. He had already served nine years of the life sentence he had picked up for severing the head from the shoulders of a rival for the favors of a lady. The severing of human heads would appear to be an odd way to start a career in nursing, but from five years of close association with him I can testify that I have never seen a kinder, more gentle-handed, and involved nurse. Ostensibly Rudolph was the hospital orderly, but he was much more than what that designation would imply. He was also nurse, expert administrator of first aid, and, after years of working closely with Dr. McDonald, an amazingly skillful—if untrained—medical man.

But Rudolph was completely illiterate, and now with the advent of the antisyphilis campaign, extensive and accurate records would have to be kept. And that is where I came in. For five years I lived and worked in close association with Rudolph, and during that time a mutual trust, respect, and friendship grew between us.

On the cold record Rudolph was a "vicious, ruthless, cold-blooded killer"—the words of the prosecutor at the time of his trial—but I knew a different side of him; my friend was a warm, compassionate man who could weep when we lost a patient for whom we had shared a ten-day, around-the-clock intensive nursing watch. The crime for which Rudolph was convicted was committed in the heat of passion; obviously he was temporarily insane at the time and had he had the money to retain a competent lawyer he would have been committed to an insane asylum for a short while until his sanity was established, and then he would have been set free. But he was poor and he was black, and the jury convicted him after only thirty minutes' deliberation; but because he was black and had killed another black man, the jury—with an attitude of, "Oh, well . . ."—had recommended mercy, thereby making a life sentence mandatory. Had he killed a white man, it would have been quite a different story. But no threat of capital punishment would have stayed Rudolph's hand; in fact at the time of his crime he was not even sure what the punishment for murder was.

It was a proud moment for me when—after I had been at the hospital for eighteen months—Rudolph christened me with the nickname Doc.

One afternoon a convict was rushed in to the hospital from the side camp at Sandy Springs suffering from an ax wound in the left thigh. It was a nasty, gaping wound, and the blow had severed an artery; the man had already lost a dangerous amount of blood, and unless that flow could be stopped quickly he was in real trouble. But Dr. McDonald could not be reached by telephone, so Rudolph and I had to do the job. When I got back to the hospital from the main office and the telephone, Rudolph had the patient on the table in the emergency room and was working on him.

"Ah cain't git hold o' that artery," he whispered, stepping aside and handing me the forceps and the curved needle threaded with catgut.

Once more my luck held: I was able to suture the artery and then close the wound with twelve stitches. As we were getting the patient into a bed and preparing him for a glucose drip, Rudolph said to me casually, "You did a good job there, Doc."

From then on I was known by that nickname in the Fulton County penal system. A convict has precious little to be proud of, and he has to latch onto little things to keep his pride alive.

In order to be more manageable the antisyphilis campaign was broken down into regional territories with a coordinator-administrator from the United States Public Health Department in charge of each territory. The administrator for the northern Georgia territory was a young woman by the name of . . . well, I came to call her Nefertiti. It was an apt name, for she had the same fine bone structure, the same look of elegant haughtiness, the same complete assurance as that possessed by that queen of ancient Egypt. Granted, I had been in prison long enough to see satin where there was calico, but under any circumstances this was quite a woman. Physically she was striking: she was slender and inordinately tall for a woman and had high cheek bones and level gray eyes. One of the things I especially remember about her was the length of the lashes which framed and accented her eyes . . . and they were not false lashes, just as nothing else about this woman was false. But above all she was intelligent.

At first I was puzzled as to why a woman as lovely as this would be involved, or interested in, the work she was doing. After I learned her story I understood.

She had completed premed and three years at the Tulane medical school when the Depression had finally wiped out her father financially. This had forced her to drop out of college and find a job to help support her family; but she had never given up her determination to become a surgeon —"And a damned good one, too"—and she was saving what money she could in preparation for the resumption of her studies.

"A couple more years . . . just a few more years . . . and Tulane, here I come!"

She had had many suitors, but she was certain marriage would put an end to her lifelong ambition, and I got the impression that because of this she was aloof in her relationships with men, especially with eligible ones, and had protectively turned herself into a loner. I suppose she allowed a very warm and close friendship to develop between us because a convict serving a life sentence was somewhat less than "eligible."

Dr. McDonald's work load was already close to the limit, and of necessity he turned the working out of the details of the campaign over to me. They seemed endless. Wassermann tests had to be run on all the present inmates of the Fulton County chain gangs, a routine system of tests on all new men at the time of their commitment had to be initiated, the blood samples had to be got into the Georgia State Health Department's laboratories in downtown Atlanta, the results of these tests had to be recorded, and a course of treatment had to be started on those with positive tests. The only specific for syphilis in those days was an arsenic compound, Salvarsan, which had to be injected directly into a vein once a week over a period of many months. The treatment was distasteful, uncomfortable, tedious, and dangerous, and as there was no law to force anyone to take treatment, many of the victims of the disease—especially the more ignorant—had to be coaxed and cajoled into submitting to the cure. The tests turned up the disturbing fact that ten per cent of the two thousand inmates had positive reactions ranging from "one plus"—the congenital form of the disease— to "four plus"—the virulent, active form.

It would have been a full-time job for one doctor to make the rounds of the six widely scattered camps to administer a weekly shot to this many patients, so we worked out a routine whereby on Saturday afternoons these men would be brought into the Bellwood Hospital for their injections, and there Dr. McDonald, Rudolph, and I administered the treatment. On most Saturday afternoons Nefertiti came out and helped us.

She had two full-time assistants, but she elected to help me, and during this period I saw her almost daily. This alone more than compensated for the long hours of work I was doing.

In order to have some understanding of my position, it is necessary to understand the peculiar form of penology that was the Georgia chain gang system of those days. A full trusty was practically a free man, about the only restriction being that he could not leave the limits of the camp in which he was confined. In my case I was answerable only to

Dr. McDonald, I had a room of my own—a tiny monk's cell off the hospital office—and Rudolph and I prepared our meals and those of the patients in the hospital kitchen. We had a small monthly food allowance for the hospital with which we could supplement the patients' chain gang rations with juices, fruit, fresh vegetables, and occasionally a piece of beef to replace the usual salt pork. Also, because I still had a few dollars left and the idiotic law of Prohibition had been repealed, I was able to keep on hand at all times a bottle of good whiskey for Rudolph and me.

Obviously a system such as this would occasionally lend itself to glaring abuses, but such instances were rare, and all in all it was a workable arrangement. For instance, two trusties who had been bookkeepers on the outside before they ran afoul of the law were working in the main office, several master carpenters were plying their trade while in prison, and the garage was employing the services of three trained mechanic trusties to work on the numerous trucks, cars, and machinery. The county was benefiting from the services of these trained men, and certainly their lives were more bearable than they would have been on the chain gang.

Soon after my transfer to the hospital I made up my mind that if this was to be my life for an undetermined number of years, I would lose myself in this life and make the best of it. And if I was to be on the fringe of medicine, I was determined to learn as much of that science as I could. Dr. McDonald soon realized I was in earnest, and he made his extensive medical library available to me.

"Here," he said one day, handing me a copy of *Gray's Anatomy*, "learn this . . . it's the basis of all medical practice."

Over the months I almost learned that vast tome by heart, and I went on then to other medical books, to the study of syndromes and symptoms, to the procedures of diagnosis and treatment. I learned as much as I could of the available medicines, of their qualities and properties, and, as in all fields of learning, the more knowledge I absorbed, the more I realized how very little I would ever really know.

After I had met and gotten to know Nefertiti, she too loaned me the books she had used at Tulane, and she and Dr. McDonald coached and chartered my course of reading.

All during this time I remembered a Molière play I had read in French class in boarding school: *Le Médecin Malgré Lui.* I'm afraid that's what I was becoming . . . a doctor in spite of myself. Undoubtedly the graybeards of the American Medical Association would have blanched had they been aware of the type of medicine Rudolph and I practiced during those years, but I don't believe we caused too much irreparable damage . . . and I like to make myself believe that we may have done some good. At least we were not amateur Doctors of Divinity—toying with men's souls.

One Saturday evening three months after the start of the campaign Nefertiti and I were sitting in my monk's cell, relaxing with some bourbon and water. It had been a particularly trying afternoon, one of those occasions when if anything can go wrong it does, and we were both in need of these relaxing drinks.

"I always enjoy coming into this tiny room of yours," she said in her exciting voice, "and seeing that print you have there on the wall." She was sitting on the side of my army surplus cot, facing a lithograph of a Meneboni horned owl that I had found someplace and which had appealed to me. Beneath it in block letters I had inscribed the adage BE NOT WISE IN THINE OWN EYES. One of the carpenters had framed it for me in a neat, narrow black frame, and it was the only decoration I had in the room.

I say *only,* for although this same trusty carpenter had lined one of the walls with bookshelves for me, I have always considered books—books which one has read and lived in for a while—as an essential part of any room in which one is to spend any time. I might have been the very antithesis of a free man, but here in prison I had carved out a refuge for myself in this small room, a place of my own to which I could retreat whenever the world got too much for me. I felt sure that Nefertiti shared my feelings about this room, that she too found in it a place where she could briefly escape from the world.

She appeared in no hurry to leave this evening, and for several hours we sat, relaxed, and talked of many things. I brought up the subject of all the many difficulties she would encounter in her efforts to make it in a field that was considered essentially man's domain.

"I know," she said, "and I think that's why this goal represents an irresistible challenge to me. A man can get by with being a mediocre doctor. But a woman? Never! I've got to become a better surgeon than any of my male associates— and I've got to do this without letting them realize this fact. For if they ever realized it they would kill me . . . they'd ruin me . . . for I would have wounded them in their silly male pride."

For a moment a wistful look came over her lovely face. "There are times when I want so badly to be just a woman . . . a wife, a mother . . . to have children of my own . . . and then I come to my senses, and I realize it wouldn't work . . . that I'd make a botch of it. You see, George, I've been bitten by this bug of my ambition . . . and it's going to ride me for the rest of my life . . ."

Suddenly she stopped and for a long moment sat looking at me with a quizzical look on her face—looking at me as though she were really seeing me for the first time.

"Do you know, George Harsh, that you and I are much alike?" she stated. "I'm driven by my ambition—and you're driven by an irresistible urge to someday know complete freedom . . . I wonder if either one of us will ever make it? But I do know this—God help the man who might marry me . . . and God help the woman who might marry you."

That evening was the first time Nefertiti and I went to

bed together. I suppose it was a classical example of two people talking themselves into bed, but we both had within us a great need, and each, in the other, found a fulfillment of this need. I was only too painfully aware of who I was—of what my position was—and she realized instinctively that the initial overture would have to come from her. This she did, simply and honestly, and for the rest of my days in prison we shared between us this warmth, this tenderness, and this momentary escape from a world we both feared might be too much for us.

9.

One day I was in the main office of the Bellwood Camp going over some commitment
papers with my friend Howell Simmons, the civilian records
clerk, when Rudolph entered and cleared his throat. "Doc,
a friend of yours has just been brang into the hospital."

By now I had got used to Rudolph's difficulty with the
verb *to bring* and, without looking up from the desk, asked,
"Who?"

"Nobie Boyles. He's got a simple fracture of the right
leg."

Nobie! I hadn't seen him in three years, and anything
bad that happened to him was not "simple" . . . and somehow Rudolph knew this. "I got a splint on it an' he's ready
to go," he added. Ordinarily on a simple fracture either
Rudolph or I would set it, feeling for juxtaposition of the
bone ends and then applying the cast. But on a friend or
relative? . . . what doctor—or pseudo doctor—ever wants to

operate on a friend or relative? It's too close, so with Howell Simmons's permission I picked up the phone and ordered an ambulance from Grady Hospital. "Let's have an X-ray on this one and get it set by professionals." Unconsciously I had used the medical *we*.

When Rudolph and I got over to the hospital I kneeled down beside the stretcher and, needlessly, verified his diagnosis of a simple fracture. Ignoring Nobie's bravado about "chicken shit, phony doctors" but noting that Rudolph had pinned the sedative tag to his shirt, I murmured as I stood up, "Tch, tch . . . it's going to have to come off . . . right below the neck."

A broad grin was spread all over his high-cheekboned, Indian face and, sticking out his hand, he laughed, "You old bastard! How are you?"

"Fine."

I suppose such laconic banalities are all that are necessary between old friends, but as I helped put him into the ambulance and after he had been driven off to Grady, I was filled with a warm glow, knowing that soon he would be back and that we would have at least a couple of weeks of renewing our friendship.

Nobie's period of convalescence was a party for all of us. Rudolph and I strained our food budget, and I reached into my own pocket in order to lay on some memorable meals. I also got in a supply of Old Grand-Dad bourbon, and when the day finally came when I could squeeze no more time out of his convalescence, we parted sadly but with our friendship glued together by bourbon whiskey.

That was the last time I saw Nobie. At a much later date I heard that he had been pardoned by Governor Rivers, that somehow he had enlisted in the paratroopers during the war, and that he had been killed on D-day during the initial paratroop drop. I am willing to run book that that great, wild half-breed Cherokee dragged a sizable number of Germans with him into the Happy Hunting Ground. No matter what he may have done in the past, in my scheme of values, society was more than repaid.

*   *   *

In prison, time is a leaden-footed, creeping bastard, but eventually it passed on into the autumn of 1940, and then things began happening at full speed.

Atlanta, because of its altitude and possibly the configuration of the mountains to the north, is periodically hit by severe ice storms. The one that paralyzed the city on this October afternoon started out as a slow drizzle. The temperature dropped rapidly, and by four o'clock the entire area was thickly covered with ice. The roads and streets were soon impassable; trees, power lines, and telephone wires were tangled together on the ground like dumped-out spaghetti, and traffic came to a standstill. One of the last vehicles on the roads that afternoon was an old Dodge touring car driven by a transfer guard bringing a sick convict from the side camp at Alpharetta to the hospital. He was an old Negro, sixty-one years of age, and his symptoms were textbook simple: he was vomiting, the right side of his abdomen was swollen and hard to the touch, he had two degrees of fever, he kept trying to pull his right knee up to his chin, and his white-cell count was crowding the moon. If that inflamed appendix was not taken out in a hurry he would not be with us for long. As soon as I ran the white-cell count I grabbed the phone that had now been installed in the hospital office and was greeted with a dead, resounding silence. Dropping the earpiece and throwing on a yellow slicker, I scurried over to the main office. Howell Simmons was sitting sideways at his desk silently peering out the window at the panorama of the storm; Max Tyree, the deputy warden, seated in a chair on the other side of the desk, was doing the same. Silently I pointed to the phone on Simmons's desk, and silently he shook his head.

"Damn," I muttered. "I got a patient over there—and

he's going to die . . . unless that appendix comes out of him."

Helplessly Simmons shrugged his shoulders. Max Tyree, taking his feet down from the window sill, reached across the desk and slowly tapped the ash from his cigar into an ashtray. Then placing the cigar in his mouth and pushing his hat back on his head, he sat for a moment silently contemplating me.

"There ain't nobody goin' nowhere," he said quietly. "There ain't no phone . . . there ain't no lights . . . there ain't no power. George . . . you're on your own."

"You mean . . . you mean . . . I got to operate?"

"I ain't said no such damn' thing. I ain't said *nothin'* to you. In fact I ain't even seen you today . . . an', Simmons, by gawd . . . you're my witness."

Taking a deep breath and turning up the collar of my slicker, I walked slowly through the pelting, freezing rain back to the hospital. "Damn . . . damn . . . damn . . . ," I mumbled with every step.

When I entered the hospital I took a quick look at the patient. Rudolph had his abdominal area packed with ice bags, and from the way the man was still trying to raise his right knee I knew the appendix had not yet burst and that we still had a chance.

"It's got to come out of there, Rudolph old buddy, and we got to do it."

I'm sure Rudolph did not turn pale—it just seemed that way—but taking a step back from the bedside, he stood for a moment with his mouth open and then, getting hold of himself, said, "Doc . . . you done lost your mind! You know what they goin' do to us if this heah niggah dies on the operatin' table? They goin' hang us!"

"Maybe he won't die . . . if we shut up and get to work."

"M-m-m, m-m-m . . . ," he muttered. "You crazy . . . an' I'm jist crazy enough to go along with you. But first we

got to have us a little sumpin' to brace us for this here
ordeal." Saying this, he disappeared into the medicine room
and was soon back with two brimming tumblers. "Here's
luck, Doc," he said as we both knocked back the ginger ale
heavily laced with medicinal alcohol. Fortunately the patient was in a state of semicoma.

We gathered up what lights we could for the operating
room: two lanterns, two flashlights, and three candles. When
we had done this I turned to Rudolph and asked him to
switch on the electric sterilizer; and he actually tried to do
so. Grinning at each other sheepishly, we got a pan of alcohol and let the instruments soak in this as we prepared the
patient for the operation. Ether was the only anesthetic we
had, and Rudolph slowly dripped some into the cone over
the patient's face as I scrubbed my hands and arms at the
sink.

"Okay, Doc . . . he's all yours."

Rudolph held one of the lanterns overhead, and I had
just made the initial incision and was fastening the clamps
when I heard him say, as though talking to himself, "Gawd
a'mighty . . . I hope he don' die."

I could feel the warmth of the grain alcohol working
through me and soothing my nerve ends. I got one finger
through the muscles, around the intestine, and gingerly
worked the swollen, pus-filled appendix to the surface. I
don't think I breathed as I tied this off, excised it, sutured it,
and carefully worked the intestine back into place. Quickly
I sutured the incision, swabbed it off, and applied the dress-
ing Rudolph had ready. Then, after we had gently placed
the patient in bed, without saying anything, we both retired
to the medicine room. I seem to recall we were on our second glass of reward when Howell Simmons stuck his head in
the door.

"I came over to see if everything is all . . . Yeah, I see
it is," he finished, grinning. "Fix me a drink of that . . .
and let me take Max one—a big one. He's chewed through

three cigars. We both been sweating this out over there . . . trying to figure out how we were going to cover this if anything went wrong. Whoosh!"

Naturally, before operating, I had given a fleeting thought to the consequences should things turn out badly; this was an unauthorized operation performed by unauthorized personnel, and should this man die because of my actions I could be held responsible. And should someone want to make an issue of it, not only would I be in trouble, but also Max Tyree and Howell Simmons, the two officials in charge of the camp at the time. There would be a grand jury investigation. Bub Clarke, as chief warden, would get involved, the county commissioners . . . but I refused to let my mind dwell on what *could* happen. The essence of the matter was that this old Negro was going to die unless I operated—this was inevitable. I did not care who he was or what he had done—he deserved at least this chance. I had seen numerous appendectomies performed, and I had assisted in many of them, and regardless of any medical profession mumbo jumbo, an appendectomy is really a simple operation. Only the peculiar circumstances made it at all difficult.

Anyway, with my luck, the whole thing turned out well, and within a month the patient was back wielding a pick and shovel. But I did sweat out the two days following the operation before Dr. McDonald could get through the ice storm to the hospital and examine the patient. After he had finished a thorough, and to my mind an unnecessarily long, examination of the patient he went into the medicine room where Rudolph and I followed him silently. For some moments, humming under his breath, he busied himself mixing one of his herb preparations.

"That was a good job you two did," he said. I started to swell like a pouter pigeon and was letting my mind dwell on the application I would file for admission to the Royal College of Physicians and Surgeons. "But, George . . . that incision. Good God . . . you weren't doing a Caesarean on an elephant, you know."

On the third day following the operation Dr. McDonald wrote a long, official report of the incident and also a personal letter addressed to the governor. I never did see the report; I think Dr. McDonald was ashamed to let me see it. Because he was a friend of mine he probably ballooned the matter out of all proportion. Taking a copy of this report and the covering letter with him, he went to see Schley Howard, my attorney, and within a week the doctor, Schley Howard, Bub Clark, and Claud Mills had an appointment with Governor Rivers. These four friends presented a very strong plea for a pardon on my behalf, and when they finished Governor Rivers, who had listened in silence, promised them that at eleven o'clock on the following morning he would give them his decision.

Accompanied by my mother, sister, and brother, Schley Howard and Claud Mills were present at the governor's office the next morning and found it filled with newspaper reporters who had been summoned by the governor. Despite the passage of years, my case, because of the supposed wealth involved, could still stir up a storm of interest. Of late there had been a dearth of sensational news, and the reporters were set to milk this story for all it was worth.

At eleven fifteen the governor appeared and, seating himself behind his desk, rapped for silence and read to the crowded room a prepared statement: ". . . one form of justice for the poor man, and one form of justice for the rich man. I hold this to be an untruth generally, and during my administration I have tried to make this an untruth specifically. In this case before us today we get to the very core of justice . . . what is justice for the poor man is justice for the rich man, and vice versa. This man has served twelve years in prison for taking a human life . . . by his recent actions he has restored a human life . . . to my mind the scales have been balanced. Thus, in my capacity as duly elected governor of the state of Georgia, I do decree, and hereby order . . ."

It was a few minutes later, amidst all the hubbub of the reporters, that my sister was able to get to a phone. Her voice was so choked by tears I could barely hear her. "We . . . we're in Governor Rivers's office . . . your . . . your pardon becomes effective tomorrow morning at seven o'clock. We'll be out to pick you up."

And then she added—almost as an afterthought—"And Rudolph has been pardoned too." I suppose an afterthought was natural enough to her, but it was no afterthought to me when I turned to this friend who was standing beside me in that prison hospital office and passed the news on to him. For a long moment we stood there silently, facing each other, and then, still without saying anything, strangely we both heaved a deep sigh. It was as though we had both finished a long race and at last could rest.

IO.

"Doc, I'm scared."

These were Rudolph's first words to me as I passed on to him the news of our pardons. And all during the rest of that busy afternoon and early evening he remained strangely quiet and thoughtful. We had much to do, there were many things to get in order before we could just walk out on these two jobs we had held for so long. At two o'clock Dr. McDonald arrived and spent the rest of the afternoon with us. At three o'clock Elmer White, the head transfer guard, brought down from the side camp at Sandy Springs the two trusties who were to be our replacements, and we had precious little time to break in these two and get them started in their new and unfamiliar jobs. Fortunately both of them were intelligent men, and by six o'clock they were as well prepared for their new duties as could be expected from anyone on such short notice. After they left, Dr. McDonald lingered for some time, and I had the impression that he was reluctant to face the final moment of good-by.

Among the three of us had grown, over the years, a trust, a respect, and a friendship that—the human condition being what it is—is rare amongst men. We were at a crossroads, the three of us, and from now on we would travel separate roads.

"Good God . . . it's late," he finally said, glancing at his watch. "I'm past due for an appointment." And then pulling himself up to his full six feet he said to us, "Thank you both . . . and good luck . . . and good-by," and, turning on his heel, he was gone. That is the way it should have been.

When Rudolph and I had finally finished everything we could do, I went into my monk's cell and got a bottle of Old Grand-Dad from my footlocker. Then we both went into the medicine room, taking a couple of straight chairs with us. Sitting down on one of the chairs, I poured two tumblerfuls of the whiskey, and for some moments we sat in silence, sipping the whiskey and smoking, both lost in our own thoughts.

"Doc, what you s'pose we goin' run into out there?"

I didn't say anything, for I had been wondering the same thing.

"I been here for fourteen years, Doc. I ain't never seen one of these talkin' pictures . . . I ain't never been on one of them buses they tell me takin' the place of street cars. I ain't never driven one of these here new cars with them fancy gear shifts . . . I ain't walked into a store in all this time and bought me nothin' . . . in all this time I ain't walked down no street with civilian clothes on . . . and they tell me they got traffic lights now . . . an' you can't walk 'cross the street 'less them lights tell you you can. How we gonna know how to act, Doc? For all this time I been tol' when to get up, when to go to bed, when to eat, when to rest, when I could smoke . . . I ain't had to do much thinkin' for myself. I ain't had to plan out my life . . . I ain't had to plan out my day . . . Doc, we goin' make fools of oursel's. Everybody gonna be pointin' at us . . . they gonna say, 'Look at them ex-convicts—they don' even know how to act' . . . They gon' laugh at us . . . an' they all gonna know where we been . . .'"

He paused then, and we both took another drink of the whiskey. I remained silent.

"I done pulled fourteen years of a black man's time, Doc," he continued, "an' you know yourself that's a lot tougher than a white man's time . . . 'cause this here's a white man's prison. An' now I got to go out into a white man's world. It ain't goin' to be too bad for you 'cause you white. But, Doc, I'm scared . . . an' you know sumpin'? . . . I got me half a mind to stay right here . . . if I could figure out some way o' doin' it."

Suddenly I remembered Dostoevski's *Crime and Punishment* . . .

". . . an' you know sumpin' else? I ain't never told you this, Doc. But when I got in this big mess I cut that niggah's head off an' I kicked it around that there room like a football . . . an' that bright-skin gal was standin' up on that bed . . . tryin' to push her back through that wall . . . and screamin' like a wounded she-cat. God a'mighty . . . if I done that once, kin I do sumpin' like that again? Doc, I'm scared."

> . . . crime is its own punishment and retributive justice can never be so severe as the penalty the human soul can impose on itself . . .

Pouring two more drinks, I recalled something Heep had once said: "What they do to us here in prison isn't really important; it's what we've done to ourselves . . . what we allow to happen within us . . ."

"I dunno, Rudolph . . . I guess you and I—and the likes of us—will carry around with us for the rest of our lives a lot of garbage in our memories. And I don't think we can ever get rid of it."

II.

"The hell with the Black Watch!" Larry said,
banging his empty glass down on the tap-
room table as though to emphasize his point. "You want to
wallow around in the mud with the likes of Curt and Pixie
and the Arkansas Ape there? Kee–rist! The stink of Curt's
cigar alone is enough to keep even a skunk out of that outfit . . ."

It was Larry Falls talking, Larry from Alabama, who had
fought in the International Brigade in Spain with the three
men of whom he was now speaking.

"Join the air force," he laughed, reaching up and patting
his own blue-clad shoulder. "Then if you get killed at least
you'll be wearing clean clothes. A clean corpse always looks
less dead anyway."

I had arrived in Montreal that morning, and now on this
first evening in that city I had made the acquaintance of

seven other Americans in the taproom of the Queen Elizabeth Hotel, where I was staying.

For six weeks following my release from Bellwood I had roamed the streets of Atlanta like a fleshed-out ghost. During these weeks I had encountered much kindness; friends of my family wanted to help, but they did not know how to, nor did I know how to accept what they did do. My brother and my sister, both of whom now had families of their own, did what they could to help me in this agonizing transition from prison life to a life of "freedom" on the outside. My mother, poor soul, seemed as lost as I was, and she was no more able to help me than I was to help myself.

It was now 1940 and America was beginning to pull its ostrich head out of the sand and arm itself. So-called defense plants of all kinds were beginning to spring up around Atlanta, but in order to find employment in one of these one had to be screened through a rigid security check. I could imagine what would happen to an ex-convict who applied for employment in one of these plants. Housing would also be needed for the army of workers to be employed in these plants, and the home-building trade was booming. There was a great need for carpenters and plumbers and masons, but a Georgia chain gang taught none of these trades. On two occasions I sought out Rudolph and we got drunk together, and I discovered he was having as much trouble making the transition as I was.

"Ah jist don' feel right around dem people what ain't been through what we been through. Ah don' know how to talk to 'em. Damn, Doc . . . what we goin' do? We jist cain't stay drunk for de rest of our lives . . ."

Then one afternoon I was approached by two friends I had known in prison. I knew them well, they had both been solid cons, they were men of rare common sense, hard business judgment, and ruthless determination. Also they were remarkably free of that hampering quality called scruples. They had both been successful bootleggers before Repeal had ruined that business, and now, by combining their forces, they had taken control of the fantastically profitable numbers racket in and around Atlanta.

"You see, we need you with us, George," Walt Cutter explained, running his large hand over his crew-cut blond hair. Walt looked more like a recent Yale graduate than he did an ex-convict, an ex-bootlegger, and now a successful gangster who had wrested control of the numbers racket.

"Yeah, Gawge," Greg Killian added, "we need yore reputation as a millionaire an' a killer . . ."

Greg was a nearly illiterate Georgia cracker who made no attempt to hide the fact, but like so many of that breed he possessed a native shrewdness and ruthlessness that would carry him far.

"What Greg means," Walt hastened to add, "is that if the thousands of people who place their bets with us everyday think they are placing these bets with a numbers outfit backed by a millionaire . . . well, do you see what it would mean? As for this 'killer' business . . . well, the three of us have been friends for a long time an' we been in prison together. We know what such reputations really are and how they're come by. But the average guy out walkin' the streets don't know this. So, let's capitalize on it.

"It's inevitable that before long some punk . . . or maybe some syndicate from up North . . . seein' all the money we're rakin' in . . . will try to horn in on our business. But I believe they'll think a long time before jumpin' in and bucking the three of us."

"Yeah, we need you, Gawge," Gregg repeated. "Come on in with us and we'll cut you in fer a full one-third share."

I didn't even put my head on my pillow that night but sat on the side of my bed smoking, lost in my thoughts. I had just been presented with a truly rare opportunity to regain with interest all the money my stupidity had cost me. The poetic justice of making society pay for the loss of my fortune and for the twelve golden years of my youth also appealed to the streak of cynicism within me. I had been in prison too long for the ethics of the matter to bother me much.

But I soon pulled my mind back from the brink of such thinking. I was under no illusions as to the real meaning behind the offer these two friends had made me: I would become a hired gun. And while my years in prison had made me contemptuous of this modern society and all its hypocrisy and greed, I still realized it was this society which made the laws and had at its disposal the means of enforcing these laws. Once before I had been on the sucker end of the deal, and I had now become too aware to again buck a system which held all the trump cards.

But I had been sorely tempted, and this thought worried me. It was time for me to take drastic action with myself. Two days later I was aboard a train bound for Montreal.

After checking into the hotel I roamed the streets all morning, fascinated by the bustle and the feeling of electric urgency in this city of a country at war. The streets were filled with colorful uniforms and flags were flying everywhere, but there was no feeling of gaiety in the air. The Canadians are a pragmatic people, a practical people with few illusions, and they had learned long ago there is nothing gay about war. I had luncheon that first day in the oak-panelled room of Drury's restaurant and had a bottle of Molson's ale with my cheddar cheese. Then I went up to the top of Mount Royal, and there the whole city and the curving St. Lawrence River was spread out below me like an aerial photograph. For several hours I sat there on the mountain, looking at the tableau spread out below me, lost in my own thoughts. Finally I came down from the mountain and, coming to the wide parklike splendor of Sherbrooke Street, I was stopped by a police barricade. For what seemed the better part of an hour I stood there bareheaded as a unit of the Black Watch marched past. This trained and combat-ready battalion was escorted by units of the various other services, and each unit had its bands, and its flags were fluttering defiantly in the breeze. The whole parade was heading for the railway station where one unit of the Black Watch would entrain for Halifax, there to board a convoy ship and head out across the ocean for . . .

There was no cheering from the crowds lining Sherbrooke Street. They stood there bareheaded, respectful, proud—and mixed in with the pride, the pride of being Canadians and the pride they felt in this column of their young men, was a quiet, fatalistic sense of sorrow. Within the living memory of most Canadians was another war, another war that had been fought such a comparatively few years ago against these same Germans, and the names Passchendaele, Vimy Ridge, Ypres—simple place names to cartographers, but to all Canadians they recalled appalling casualty lists. People remembered that the entire male population of whole towns and villages had been wiped out in the battles named after crossroads on a map. There was nothing romantic or glamorous about war to this nation of twelve million people; only one generation before, they had been bled white by a war, and now, once more, they were being asked to lay their blood on the line. There was no cheering from the crowds lining Sherbrooke Street.

It was now five o'clock in the afternoon, and going back to my hotel, I found a quiet corner in the dark cocktail lounge, where I composed my soul and prepared it for an uninterrupted evening of solitary boozing. I was on my third glass of Dewar's and water, my third milepost on what promised to be a monumental drunk, when seven men in a group entered the lounge and sat down at a large round table next to mine. Three of them wore the khaki tunics and kilts of the wartime Black Watch, two of them were in air force blue uniforms, and two were in civilian clothing. There was something formidable-looking, rugged, about all seven of them, but one in particular would have stood out in a herd of charging elephants. He was a huge man, a mountain of a man, and his hairy, gaitered legs sticking out from his kilt looked like twin oak trunks. A huge cigar was jutting out of one corner of his mouth, and he was simultaneously belching out a torrent of words and billowing clouds of cigar smoke. Reaching up, he snatched off his tam from his nearly bald head and, tossing it onto the center of the table, he fumbled for a moment in his breast pocket with a hand the size of a Smithfield ham.

"Twenty dollars!" he boomed, tossing a wad of bills into the tam. "Twenty bucks . . . that's the price of admission . . . the entrance fee to this night of drinking! Step right up, gents . . . ante up and get separated from the boys!"

"Everybody gets drunk!" he laughed. "But goddam, Ape," he added, turning to the man sitting next to him, "this time, when we get back to camp, keep your southern, grits-packin' mouth shut, will ya?" Then turning to the others at the table as though appealing to a jury, he asked, "Y'know what this Arkansas Ape did the last time we got bottled? I know a hole in the fence around in the back of the camp—a hole we can crawl through and get by with coming back late from pass— and I'm tryin' to lead this clown around there and keep him quiet—we're already two hours awol—but what does this joker do? He throws back his head, lets out a scream of rage, and bellows that only chickens and nigrahs crawl under fences where he comes from! Naturally the MPs hear us . . . we spent two days in the brig on that one."

Later on, after I got to know these men, I learned that Curt, the Arkansas Ape, and Pixie—a gnomelike man with pointed ears who had been an associate professor of philosophy at NYU before deciding to go forth and tilt with windmills—had been in the International Brigade in Spain together before teaming up once more in the Black Watch. Larry Falls, the Alabaman, had also been in Spain with them, as had a beardless youth who had somewhere picked up the nickname The Worm. But these latter two had joined the RCAF instead of the Black Watch, and because of this they were almost considered deserters by the three foot soldiers.

"Dropping bombs on people's heads!" Pixie, the philosophy professor, frequently scolded them. "Tch, tch! How would you like someone to do that to you? You could get shot for doing things like that."

"Maybe so," Larry laughed, "but I've had enough of eating mud with you three guys—Spain cured me of my appetite for mud—and dust. This time I'm going to war like a gentleman . . . with clean fingernails. And besides—look at Curt's belly . . . I don't like people stickin' bayonets in me. I'm ticklish."

Later, when I saw the massive scar across the expanse of Curt's stomach, I realized why all of these men who had been in Spain together took a proprietary pride in that scar. It was as though he wore this great angry-looking welt across his midriff as a battle badge, a unit citation of which all of them could be proud. Knowing something of the suturing of torn human flesh and seeing that scar, I was convinced that whoever had sewn up this wound had done so with a length of grapevine. But what raised this scar above the status of the ordinary was the legend that had been tattooed above it: OPENED BY MISTAKE.

It soon became known that I too was an American, and in no time I had made my contribution to the kitty and was swept up in the party. The memory of much of that evening is understandably cloudy, but toward the end, close to midnight, something occurred that sobered me as though the entire icy torrent of Niagara Falls had been dumped onto my head.

I was sitting next to a man from Knoxville, Chuck Leach. The lines on his face gave him the expression of a hounddog; but around his eyes were etched crow's-feet of laughter. After a long speculative moment he asked, amidst the hubbub of the party, "Where did you pull your time?"

Putting the cigarette I had been lighting into an ash tray,

I sat for some moments silently and slowly stirred the drink before me with a swizzle stick. What had I said, what had I done, what telltale mark was there on me that had allowed this man to see my secret?

"Georgia," I said at last," . . . the chain gang . . . twelve years."

"Jesus!" he muttered, shaking his head.

And then I knew. There is no scar, there is no mark, there is no brand—there is no outward sign or symbol for the world to see. But there is something that allows one man who has served long years in prison to recognize instinctively another human being who has had a similiar experience.

"Where did you pull yours?" I asked.

"Tennessee . . . the Brushy Mountain Coal Mine . . . five years."

"Jesus!" I muttered, shaking my head.

From then until his death a short time later, neither he nor I again mentioned our pasts, but the knowledge we shared deepened our friendship and the feeling of respect we had for each other.

By now the party had really gathered momentum, and Pixie, he with the pointed ears, had been persuaded to sing. In a clear, bell-like tenor he led with the solo part of a song that was obviously a favorite of this group, and the others would crash in with the chorus:

> *O-o-h, cats on the rooftops,*
> *Cats on the tiles,*
> *Cats with the syphilis,*
> *Cats with the piles!*
> *Cats with their ahse holes*
> *   wreathed in smiles,*
> *As they revel in the joys of copulation!*

That did it. The assistant manager of the hotel, the maitre d', and four waiters converged on us, and after some discussion it was firmly suggested we go elsewhere. Curt, puffing cigar smoke like an old wood-burning locomotive, said he knew of a bottle club that stayed open all night, and like a convoy following a man-of-war, most of the group at the table followed him out the door.

My conversation with Chuck had done much to sober me, and I had had enough for one evening. Chuck had also declined the offer to go along, saying that he had to report early in the morning to air force headquarters to be formally sworn in, and was now ordering a pot of coffee from the dubious waiter.

"Now," said Chuck, pouring out two cups of coffee, "now we can get down to the nuts and bolts of this business. Do you want to get into the air force?"

"Sure . . . but I was afraid I was going to have a tough time getting into even the Black Watch. D'you really think I can make the air force?"

"Nothing to it"—he grinned—"I made it . . . you can make it. First: you're up here, so obviously you've got your birth certificate with you. I don't suppose you brought a high school diploma with you? No, well, neither did I. So, you'll be given the same educational test that I was . . . there's nothing to it, really. The only tough part of this thing is the physical exam. All air crew members are volunteers—that is, the applicants for pilots, navigators, wireless operators, and gunners—and you'd be amazed at how many of these guys volunteering can't pass the physical. These people are having a tough time filling their needs."

"I'm not worried about that part of it," I said soberly. "What worries me is . . ."

"Well, to start with they don't fingerprint you . . . but I know what you're talking about." Chuck laughed. "And this is probably your first time to face that one—'Have you ever been convicted of a felony?' Well, believe me, I've lost out on some good jobs because of that one. And it's one that'll haunt you for the rest of your life . . . no matter what you do. But up here—and right now, it's different. I honestly don't think they can afford to be too particular. They're fighting with their backs to the wall—they're desperate. So, when you come to that one in the four-page questionnaire that they'll throw at you first, just take a deep breath and put down a big, fat NO. It won't be the last time you'll have to lie in order to eat, y'know. But anyway, that's what I did ten days ago . . . and tomorrow I'm being sworn in. You'll make it. In the morning come down to the air force recruiting center with me, and I'll get you started in the right line anyway."

12.

I was finally accepted as a volunteer candidate for air crew by the Royal Canadian Air Force, but not until I had argued my way past the age limitation. Chuck had prepared me for this.

"Twenty-eight is the age limit for pilots, navigators, radio operators, and gunners . . . and there's no way of doctoring these birth certificates. But if your marks are good enough in the tests—the educational tests, the I.Q., but especially the physical—they'll close their eyes to these few years. But be prepared to argue."

I passed all my tests without any trouble, especially the physical exam, in which a fact about me was uncovered of which I had been unaware: I had phenomenal night vision, almost that of a cat, and this fact alone—regardless of my preference—would shunt me into Bomber Command. Almost all bombing done by the RAF was night bombing, and of course good night vision was a valuable asset. But unfortunately when I reached the admissions officer I ran into a book-stickler. If the book said twenty-eight was the age limit, then twenty-eight it was, and there was no use in discussing the matter. He had all my papers spread out on the desk before him, and one by one I went through those papers, pointing out to him the marks I had made and laying special stress on my newly discovered cat's eyes, but I might as well have been using my breath to blow up balloons—at least then I would have had something to show for my efforts. He remained adamant. Despite his rank of flying officer, or first lieutenant, he was a ground officer, and he used this opportunity to point out the great service the ground officers were rendering in the RAF.

"For every one who flies," he pointed out to me, "the services of ten other people on the ground are required to keep that one aloft." As he talked I noticed he was busily doodling on a pad of paper on the desk before him. The doodle was a mathematical equation he was working on.

I was about to launch into another plea when an older man entered the room. The flying officer behind the desk almost lost his glasses in his haste to jump up and come to attention, but the older man waved at him to be seated.

"Carry on, Haskins," he said in an exaggerated British drawl. "What's all the nattering going on in here? I heard part of it in my office next door."

As Haskins presented his side of the case I had a chance to study the older man. He was in air force blue, and on the sleeves of his tunic were the four stripes of a group captain, or colonel, but what immediately impressed me were the spread wings of the old Royal Flying Corps of World War I sewn to the breast of the tunic. Beneath the wings he wore a single ribbon—the blue-and-white diagonally striped ribbon of the Distinguished Flying Cross of the RAF. This single ribbon told the whole story—there was no need for any others. As anyone who has ever flown in combat can attest, anyone wearing that ribbon was a bona fide hero.

"H-m-m . . ." he kept repeating to himself as he went through my papers on the desk. Haskins continued his nattering, but I don't think this man even heard him. Finally, having finished reading the papers, he looked at me for a long moment, and I had a distinct feeling of being sized up.

"Come into my office, old boy," he said to me, not even glancing at Haskins.

Following him into his office, I stood respectfully in front of his desk as he seated himself behind it. "Good man, Haskins, really," he drawled. "Queen Victoria would have been proud of him. On such servants has the empire been founded." He pronounced it "empah." "But when it comes to war . . . well, they're rather lacking in imagination, I'm afraid. Just what branch of air crew did you wish to volunteer for, old boy?"

"Air gunner," I heard myself say.

Somehow I think the words I had just blurted out startled me even more than they surprised the group captain, for I don't recall having had any conscious desire at that time to get into this war as an air gunner. I recalled Chuck telling me of several other Americans who had volunteered as air gunners because it would enable them to get overseas with the minimum delay, and I also remember him speaking of the high mortality rate among gunners. But I think there had been rambling around in the back of my mind some half-formed notion that I would become a Spitfire pilot, a hard-drinking, dashing figure with a white silk scarf wrapped around my neck, the almost unbearable strain and demands of my job etched deeply into my face.

There suddenly entered my mind with icy clarity an awareness of exactly what I was trying to do: in one flamboyant *beau geste* I was trying to counterbalance my entire past. I had become a glory hunter. I was a man who was trying to prove something, and the sorry history of man's endeavor on this planet is one long testament to the amount of mischief such a man can cause. Napoleon was trying to prove that a little man could raise as much hell as a big six-footer; Hitler was trying to prove the superiority of the Aryan race (whatever that is), and DeGaulle spent the declining years of his life trying to prove that Roosevelt and Churchill were wrong in laughing at him and his pretensions to *la Gloire*. All of history bears out this theory, and there I was, in my petty little way, trying to prove something. I was trying to prove that "they" were wrong when "they" sentenced me to hang, I was trying to prove that "they" were wrong when "they" passed a law barring ex-convicts from the armed services, but most of all, I was trying to prove myself, trying to prove to my own satisfaction that I really belonged in this world as a full member of a society that had once expelled me. And I could legally. No, there is nothing more dangerous in this world than a man who is trying to prove something, for such a man is unsure of himself, he is a mass of quavering self-doubts, and he will do anything, make any play to the grandstand, to still this uncertain voice he hears within himself. His is indeed the uncertain trumpet.

I think now, had I been that group captain, I would have made certain that such a man be armed with nothing more lethal than a potato-paring knife and be relegated for the duration of the war to performing kitchen-police duties in some army camp in the wilds of Saskatchewan. Instead he said, after looking at me sharply for a moment, "Well, there shouldn't be any problem there."

And there wasn't. In three days' time I was sworn in as a member of His Britannic Majesty's Armed Forces, and in so doing I forfeited my United States citizenship, the same citizenship that had only recently been restored to me with my pardon; at the time I realized that someday this would present a problem for me, but I would worry about that when the time came. And besides, if I didn't come back from the war . . . well, it just was not worth worrying about at that time.

With a contingent of thirty-six other volunteers I was sent to an aerial gunnery school in Ontario, close to Niagara Falls. Early in the morning of our departure from Montreal we were assembled in the street outside air force headquarters, and the sight of such a ragtag gaggle of disparate civilians would have warmed the hearts of Hitler and his trained Wehrmacht could they have seen it. On the march to the railway station—during which we made a brave attempt to maintain some semblance of military demeanor—I had a chance to observe my fellow volunteers; not more than three or four of them appeared old enough to vote, and once more I was made aware of the historical fact: old men don't fight wars, they just declare them. Because of my age and the gray hairs that were beginning to show, I soon became known among my companions as Pop.

The three months' training at the gunnery school was intense, concentrated, and thorough. The first three weeks were devoted to converting us from civilians into reasonable facsimiles of soldiers; we were taught the British manual of arms, close-order drill, and we spent hours on the rifle ranges and in bayonet practice. We were taken on forced-route marches, and we bivouacked overnight in the mud and the rain; we worked twelve hours a day, seven days a week, and never for a moment were we allowed to forget that there was a war on; but above all we learned the basis of all military discipline—blind, unquestioning obedience to an order. At the end of these first three weeks we went on into the main purpose of our training. We learned the vast difference between the aerial firing of machine guns and the ground firing of these same weapons. We learned about vectors and parabolas of fire and arcs of fire and cones of fire. We learned about machine guns and the care of them and the clearing of stoppages in sub-zero temperature with bare hands. We learned about gun turrets and the hydraulic power that operated them, but beyond all else we were trained in the art of firing machine guns and hitting what we were shooting at. Once again the thought struck me—as it had so often during my prison years—that I seemed to be picking up an inordinate number of skills that would be utterly worthless to me should I ever earn my freedom. When the course was over I discovered, to my surprise, that I was top man in the class. Apparently some sort of strange affinity existed between me and machine guns.

It just happened that the second highest man in the class was also an American—John J. Kerr Caskie of Warrenton, Virginia. John was of that small tribe of men around whom legends grow in their own lifetimes. Tall, handsome, obviously from a family of wealth, and possessed of an amazing education . . . on the surface the world would appear to be his private oyster . . . but John wanted no part of the world's standards of success. He was still in his mid-twenties, but one got the impression that he had seen it all, and wanted no part of it. Impressions were about all one got of John, for while he was a free and interesting talker, he rarely spoke of himself or his own personal history; therefore, I suppose he was a slightly different man to each one of us who got to know him and to cherish his friendship. There were those who were sure John was carrying a torch—that he had been disappointed in love and that he was using the RCAF as some sort of romantic Foreign Legion. But after I got to know him I came to realize that any such self-dramatizing would be utterly contradictory to his nature; he had too keen a sense of the ridiculous and was too busy laughing at himself to ever fall into the role of a self-pitying romantic.

I was sure that all his life John had found things too easy for him, that things had always been handed to him, and that finally he had made up his mind to do something on his own. Somewhere along the various paths of his life he had picked up an amused and tolerant cynicism regarding mankind and all its petty posturings and pretensions. But his cynicism was relieved of any viciousness or bitterness because he himself was the principle target of his laughter.

John also possessed a "photographic mind." On occasion one of his friends would ask him to read a long paragraph from a book; he would do this silently and then, handing the book back to one of us, quote the entire paragraph verbatim. It was no wonder he had an amazing education—studying must have been a snap for him.

But with all his gifts, and all his attributes, and all his lovable qualities I don't believe John really much cared whether he lived or died. He appeared to be completely disillusioned with mankind and the type of society man has evolved for himself, and when he finally died—a young man —I don't believe it mattered much to him. With his last breath he probably found something to laugh at in his own demise.

Following the completion of our training, the procedure was that out of the top six men in the class two would be selected for commissions. This selection was done in a peculiarly British manner: these six men would present themselves in a group before a board of examining officers, and after a brief oral examination each one on his own would be required to stand at ease and discourse for twenty minutes on any subject under the sun. This is no simple chore, as anyone who has tried it can testify, but reasonable sanity prescribed that this talk should be confined to the principles and practices of aerial gunnery.

But this was not for John. He started out slowly, lucidly, and rationally, but knowing him and the way his mind worked, I unconsciously braced myself for whatever might be coming. And it was not long before it came. Like a hunter enticing his prey into a trap, John lulled this board of officers into a semi-somnolent state with a tedious recital of what he had recently learned, and then gradually he worked his way into a detailed description of a new Japanese fighter plane, the Mitisigawa, which had retractable wings for flying through tunnels and fired rice pellets which had been soaked overnight in a special preparation of stemmick water and slitvick acid, which enabled them to penetrate ocklesteen feet of armor plate, provided the armor plate was made of a secret type of ape shit, bull shit, bits and pieces out of the King's Regulations for Air Force, and any other bits of idiocy found lying about . . .

For twenty-five minutes John kept up this masterly flow of double talk. While I listened to John my eyes were on the officers of the board, watching the changing expressions come over their puzzled faces. One older officer, apparently believing that his ears had gone crazy, dug at his right ear with his forefinger and then, cocking his head, sat with this ear pointing toward the "speaker." With the skill of an accomplished artist John wove his Jabberwockian tapestry together, interspersing intelligible phrases with long bursts of sheer nonsense and near-words, so that after a moment or two of this the hearers were in a state near panic, convinced their reason had deserted them.

John wound up his peroration by thanking his listeners for their jubitilly picosational and sat down—amid thundering silence. Had I been a member of that board I would have commissioned John on the spot; but instead he wound up his career in the RCAF as a sergeant gunner.

As a result of this board meeting and my marks in the gunnery school I was awarded a commission, and two days later I held the rank of pilot officer in His Majesty's Royal Air Force. At the ceremonial parade held for this purpose I was called before the squadron, and the royal commission was read to me: "We, George the Sixth, King of England, Ireland, Scotland, and the Dominions beyond the Seas, Emperor of India, Defender of the Faith . . . reposing special faith in our trusty and well-beloved George Harsh, do hereby . . ."

As this imposing document was read to me I could have sworn that I saw the incredulous face of Boss Bray and those of several other of my erstwhile acquaintances peeping out from the clouds overhead.

After being given a dollop of pay, a uniform allowance, a traveling allowance, and a per diem allowance, I was given ten days' "overseas" leave, and I met my mother and my sister in New York. I was dressed in my new tailor-made uniform, and the pride my mother now took in me made the whole effort seem worthwhile; one could almost see her swell as she was able to introduce me as "My son, the RAF pilot officer." It was the last time I was to see her alive, and I have always been grateful that I was able to do this small thing for her toward the end.

John soon learned part of the annoying price he was going to have to pay for having kicked a commission in the teeth, for while he was transported to England in an overcrowded troopship, I, along with eleven other officers, made the voyage in comfort aboard a fast, armed merchantman that had been taken over by the Royal Navy.

Our ship docked in Grennock, Scotland, and the twelve of us trooped ashore. We had been fed an early breakfast, and as it was now eleven o'clock we decided to kill the hour before our train left for the south by having some coffee—and hopefully, coffeecake—in a dockside restaurant. Without being especially conscious of it, I was carrying in my hand a large Florida orange that I had saved from my breakfast, and as we sat down at a table the waitress, a pleasant-looking Scottish woman, spied the orange, and a look came over her face as though she were seeing the gates of heaven.

"An orange," she said quietly, as though speaking to herself. "An orange," she repeated with awe in her voice.

"Would you like to have it?" I asked, holding it out to her.

"Oh, sir," she quavered and the tears stood in her eyes. "Oh, sir . . . my little boy . . . he's three . . . and he's never seen an orange . . ."

"Christ," I thought to myself, "an orange . . ." But somehow I've never forgotten that small incident that was my introduction to the British Isles in wartime.

It's a long train ride from Grennock in Scotland down to Bournemouth on the south coast of England, and there is not much I remember about it except, during the daylight hours, looking out the window and frequently seeing the charred reminders of the air raids that had skipped hardly an English town of any size. But of course the American and Canadian papers and magazines had been filled with photographs taken during the blitz, and I don't think this firsthand evidence of what bombs can do to real estate shocked any of us greatly. From the train window one couldn't see the blood and the tears. Certainly none of what I saw moved me as much as that Scottish woman, her little boy, and the orange.

Bournemouth is an old and beautiful resort city filled with luxury hotels, and the RAF had taken over several of these as billeting quarters. There we would be stationed until we could be sorted out and sent on to various other places for our further training. I was assigned a small, stripped-down room in one of these hotels, a room overlooking the sea and the Isle of Wight in the distance, and I settled in for the waiting that seems an inevitable concomitant of any war. It was a pleasant two weeks that I spent in a pleasant city. Every morning there would be an early parade and roll call during which the day's orders were read, and then we were free to spend the rest of the day as we pleased. As a boy I had been in England and had got to know and love the country, but of course that had been in peacetime, and I was now having to adjust to wartime conditions, to the blackouts, the shortages, the restrictions, and the belt-tightening rationing. It seemed rather odd to me that under these conditions, and with the acute manpower shortage, that I, a junior officer, should be assigned a batman; but apparently this custom originated back in the days of Camelot, and no one would ever think of changing it. As a concession to the times the services of this batman were spread rather thin. He attended to ten of "his young gentlemen." Like a mother hen he watched over us, made our beds, shined our shoes, polished our brass buttons, and was guide, mentor, and guardian to the lot of us. He was a wizened little man in his late fifties and his name was Clatter and I loved him. He was a pessimist in reverse—if there is such a thing—for he operated on the theory that never could anything be as bad as he dreaded and predicted that it would be. Every morning he would "knock us up" with a cup of tea and an unvarying ritual: " 'ere you are, suh . . . a bit of tea. It ayn't as 'ot as I'd like hit to be . . . an' if yer don't like it sweet, don't stir hit. Shockin' news this mornin', suh. Birmin'ham got blitzed proper last night, hit did. The press and wireless is filled with hit . . . 'undreds got killed, they did. A proper mess. An' the news from North Africa hayn't a' tall good. Gettin' a bit o' smashin' about there, we are. But good mornin' to ya, suh, and 'ave a good day!"

It was very pleasant and civilized to lie there in bed for those few minutes every morning, stretching and enjoying a cup of tea and the first cigarette of the day and feeling certain that things just couldn't be as bad as Clatter had depicted them. Most of my life I have enjoyed those first few moments of any day, the moments after first awakening, for one's world is fresh and the slate is clean. At that time the day is before us to do with as we can. No one has yet had time to do anything dastardly, mean, contemptible, or outrageous to us, and conversely we in our turn have not yet had time to do anything dastardly, mean, contemptible, or outrageous to anyone else. It's a good time of day. It's a good time for making resolutions which last until one has had one's first cup of coffee.

Anyway, it was during one of these resolution-making morning intervals that I resolved to give up cigarettes for a pipe. This decision was not made for health reasons, for I have always been able to present a rather convincing argument that someday I'm going to die of something anyway, but rather because a life of awakening to an English war-time cigarette was just not a life worth awakening to. On the other hand, the pipe tobacco available was up to normal standards. I don't suppose this is to be marvelled at, considering that England is predominantly a pipe-smoking country. In England I learned that a pipe is not merely an instrument from which one draws sensual pleasure; it is also an adjunct to diplomacy, a cover-up for a vacant mind, and an admirable aid in keeping one's mouth shut. With a pipe stuck in one's mouth and an occasional noncommittal *m-m,* one can gain the reputation of having the wisdom usually attributed only to owls.

After several days John Caskie and his torpedo-harassed convoy of troops also arrived, and we were posted to our various squadrons. John was posted to a squadron flying four-engined Lancasters, and I, after six or seven operational missions with another squadron, was posted to 102 Squadron of Four Group in Bomber Command as squadron gunnery officer. It seems rather useless now, useless and repetitious, to write of my experiences during the months I was an operational airman flying combat missions. The whole period, looking back on it, is one strung-together mishmash of times during which I was either half-drunk or half-terrified, and sometimes I was both together. The English Channel in the moonlight always looked to me like a vast expanse of cold, scalloped grease, and the mud flats of Holland always looked like the black fingers of an extended hand stretching out to ensnare and pull down the unwary. Once we winged in over those mud flats I started bracing myself for what I knew would be coming—and it never failed me. Those first few moments of crossing over the coastline of Holland were always the worst, for the memories of England, the comforts of the mess, the laughter and the companionship of beautiful women, and all the other trappings and rewards of the good and civilized life were still fresh in one's mind.

And then it would come—the glaring, probing fingers of

the searchlights and then the flak. With the first bursts the fear, the sweating, and the good memories would vanish, and one became a cold, efficient machine, the unthinking automatic extension of the four-banked Browning guns.

Although I knew flak was as deadly as a coiled cobra, I never got over marveling at the beauty of it. The arcing and coiling paths of the tracer shells coming from the rapid-firing Bofors guns looked like the fiery balls coming from a Roman candle. The heavier bursts and crumps of the flak flashed red, yellow, purple, and green; and the eerie, ghostly glow of the searchlights wavered through the whole mass and lighted up the drifting clouds of smoke. Sitting there awed by the lethal beauty of the antiaircraft fire, I used to have the insane sensation of feeling sorry for those mortals who would never witness such a display of wild beauty. Crazy? I have often wondered how far the mind would reach to protect, shield, and cloak itself from a reality that might otherwise be too dreadful to bear.

But the flak was an impersonal thing, a general malevolence directed against the entire heavens. The night fighters were something else; they had one's name, rank, and number engraved on their bullets. Suddenly the flak would be cut off, and the blackness of the night would enfold the sky, and you would know the night fighters were coming in. The voices in the intercom would crackle off to silence, and in earphones could be heard the short, heavy breathing of the other crew members as they sat tensed, waiting. And then you'd see it—the blacker shape against the black night like the shape of a shark swimming up out of the depths, and you'd see it maneuvering, shifting position, getting ready for its run in, the initial pass that would have to knock out the rear turret. And slowly, steadily, smoothly, and without jerking, as you had been trained to do, you'd swing the turret around, and you'd hear the hum of the hydraulics as you lifted the guns with the control stick and brought the gun sight to bear. You'd get his shape in the center of the orange, glowing circle within the sight, and you wouldn't look directly at that black shape, but you'd look off to one side of it, holding it in your peripheral vision. You were ice water now because you had been trained to be ice water. And you'd sit there. And you'd see his shape loom larger in your gun sight, and soon his wing tips would fill the entire orange, glowing circle, and you'd know that now—*now* he's in range! And every nerve in your body would be screaming and shouting, "Now! Now! Jesus God in Heaven . . . Now! Mash your thumb down on that firing button! NOW! Make those four Brownings roar and buck and jump . . . oh, God! Let me smell the stink of burning cordite!" But you'd sit—because you'd been trained to. Let him have the first shot. Let his wing tips suddenly light up with his fire, and try not to pay any attention to his burst of tracers flying past you like a flock of red-hot pokers. Let him have the first shot, for that would give you the slight, split-second advantage. The bucking from his four cannons and eight machine guns would throw off his first aim, and because his aircraft itself was his gun sight, he would have to waste a couple of precious seconds in maneuvering his plane back onto target, and those seconds were yours. Now—now was your moment—and as you gritted your teeth your thumb would bear down on that black firing-button, the chattering roar of those sweet Brownings would fill the turret, and playing it like a lethal fire hose, you'd pour that cone of fire into the nose of the Messerschmidt 110, play it all over him—in short bursts to be sure you were hitting him—play it over the Plexiglas of his cockpit, onto the leading edges of his wings to get fuel tanks, but above all blast it right into his face. And then, if through some miracle he was still there, he would get his second chance at you. But by now, because of the speed of his closing, he would only have time for a short burst before he would have to break off, and then would come your real chance. His best breakoff maneuver would be a fast diving-turn to starboard that would carry him beneath you and give you only the most awkward shot, but for some reason—probably the ostrich instinct that what we don't see won't hurt us—nine out of ten times he would break off in a climbing-turn that would expose his ugly, oil-streaked belly to you. And if you missed that one you should turn in your wings and apply for a job peddling hot pork pies on the beach at Brighton.

You had him then, and the only problem was to do the job with the least possible expenditure of ammunition. And as he fell off in a blazing coffin and plummeted to earth in a series of fluttering swoops, you didn't even have time to speculate as to whether this man you had just killed was named Karl or Franz or Werner or Gerhardt . . . you had to clear that stoppage in the number three gun, cock it, and get set for the next one—for one thing was certain: Karl or Franz or whoever had not been out there alone.

Then once more you would cross over the mud flats of Holland, out over the cold, scalloped Channel, only this time you were heading for home, and in the first gray light of dawn you would pass over Flamborough Head, and you would know you had made another one. The reaction would set in now, the cold feeling that seemed to nestle up against your bones. The trembling would start, and you knew that you were passing through that invisible barrier, that your mental gears were reshifting, and that you were rejoining the human race.

In all honesty I cannot say that during that period when I was actively engaged in this orgy of killing that I felt any sense of personal guilt for my acts, nor—in that same spirit of honesty—can I claim that today my sleep is disturbed by nightmares, that I wake up in the middle of the night screaming, or that I am growing hollow-eyed from lack of sleep. I have heard others with backgrounds and experiences similar to mine claim that this does indeed happen to them. It may—who am I to say not?—but upon hearing this, I always have the suspicion that the speaker may be sticking his tongue in his cheek, perhaps telling his listeners what he thinks they would like to hear, or he may be indulging himself in a bit of that self-dramatization in which we all love to wallow at times.

As the dawn began to break over the fields of England I would, with cold and trembling fingers, fumble amidst the straps and buckles and flaps of my flying gear and extract the flask of brandy from my hip pocket and take a long, gurgling belt of this time-tested restorative.

Soon, having found and circled over our home base, we spotted the operations officer standing at the end of the runway and signaling with his green Aldis lamp the call letters of our squadron and aircraft—B, Y, O for orange—and with the four magnificent Merlin Rolls-Royce engines straining against the lowered flaps, we would settle in for the touch down. Then, having taxied to the dispersal site, we shut off the engines and the sudden silence tore at our ear drums. Then, one by one, we would drop out of the hatch and walk slowly over to the waiting lorry. The birds would just be starting their cheerful greetings to this new day, and for some reason the sound always startled me, as though I thought those birds had no right to be any part of this crazy business. And yet I loved that sound, for I knew they were English birds and that once again I was on friendly soil.

The same WAAF would be standing beside her lorry waiting for us with a big cheerful smile on her English-complexioned face, the same WAAF who had seen us off the night before and had watched unconcernedly as we each in turn had unbuttoned and peed on the port wheel for luck. The night before as we had taxied out of the dispersal site she had seen us off with that big smile and her arm held aloft and her fingers giving the victory sign, and this morning the smile was still there and so was her unvarying greeting: " 'Morning, chaps. Have a nice trip?"

And the reply would come from my polite British fellow crew members, as though we had just returned from a holiday cruise to the Caribbean, "Veddy nice, thenk you."

Well, these were some of the aspects of the active war as I knew it during that winter of 1941 and the spring and summer of 1942. Of the good moments I especially remember the leaves I spent with Michele, an English girl whose husband had been a captain in the tank corps in the Libyan desert. We found each other shortly after she had received her telegram from the War Ministry informing her that her husband, who had previously been reported missing, must now be presumed dead. That is the cruelest telegram of all, for it leaves ajar the door of hope, and the final adjustment to the inevitable can never be made. We found each other when we were both in need of what the other had to offer— tenderness, kindness, and a reassurance that the entire world wasn't mad. All during that spring, summer, and fall that we shared I don't think Michele ever really faced up to that telegram: we would be walking down a street together, and suddenly I would feel her arm stiffen and her pace quicken, and looking up, I would see a tank corps officer in his black beret approaching us, and then, as he neared us, I could feel the disappointment slacken her arm. And at night, on occasions, I could hear her whispering softly in her sleep, and I knew what was in her heart.

It was shortly after I met Michele that I received word of Chuck Leach's death. Chuck, now a commissioned Spitfire pilot, had finally caught up with John Caskie and me, and the three of us had spent many of our leaves together. Between the three of us we had drunk many a private bottle club dry during a night. All during the time I knew him I don't think Chuck quite got over marveling at the weird turn his fortune had taken. This was especially true the night we three celebrated his being awarded the Distinguished Flying Cross. He had been summoned to Buckingham Palace for a formal presentation, and the king himself had pinned the medal on his chest that afternoon. The queen had been there, as had Princess Elizabeth and Princess Margaret Rose. There had been a band and a parade, and the sun had shone, and for once the Luftwaffe had behaved itself and not spoiled the party with a stick of bombs.

After all this pomp and ceremony and scarlet and gold Chuck was badly in need of the drink we had waiting for him at Jack Doyle's club. Jack was also in on the celebration and wouldn't let any of us buy a drink that night. Jack Doyle, "The Irish Thrush" of pugilistic fame, had once lasted one full round with the champion, Max Baer. He had a warm spot in his heart for most Americans, and this was understandable, considering the amount of easily earned loot he carried out of Madison Square Garden following that high point of his prizefighting career.

As it turned out, that wild night was the last time Chuck, John, and I were ever to be together again, and it was such a night as I am sure Chuck would have wanted it to be. It was on this night that John gained for himself the nickname that was to stick to him for the time remaining until his death.

Shortly after our arrival in England John J. Kerr Caskie of Warrenton, Virginia, presented himself in civilian clothing at the staid premises of Gieves, Ltd. in Bond Street in London. This venerable tailoring firm had made the uniforms for the Duke of Wellington, Lord Nelson, and field marshals too numerous to list, but this would be the first time they had tailored a uniform for a sergeant in the Royal Air Force. After much hemming and hawing and considerable hrrrumphing, and because John had not only the cash but also the necessary clothing coupons, they agreed to make the uniform . . . and they made it to his specifications. On the outside, with the exception of the cloth from which it was made, it was a regulation uniform. But once it was turned inside out it became something quite different. The tunic was fully lined with red satin, and it was an exact replica of the uniform of a subaltern in Lord Howe's army when that British force landed in Boston following the Tea Party. From then on, whenever John looked on the wine when it was too red, he would become a turncoat, and standing at some bar in London, he would quote in rolling phrases the corny, "empah"-extolling poetry of Rudyard Kipling, or discourse at length on the "uppity colonials who failed to appreciate the yoke of British imperialism." The Englishmen of those days were too sure of themselves to mind having their legs pulled.

On this particular night, during which John created his own nickname, six or seven of us were sitting in Jack Doyle's, doing our utmost to exhaust Jack's supply of scotch. Chuck had just said that the only thing about that afternoon of pomp that had had any reality to him had been the unicorn of the British seal emblazoned on a wall in the palace, and we were all drinking to the reality of the unicorn and to the health of all unicorns generally when John, with his tunic reversed, strode to the bar and slammed his open hand down on the mahogany surface with a resounding thump. In the ensuing silence he raised his voice and shouted, "My name's O'Toole . . . any sonofabitch in the house can whip me!"

From then on—from that variation of John L. Sullivan's alcoholic boast—John was known as The O'Toole to those of us who knew and loved him.

But all of this is just a piece of the entire mad crazy quilt of jumbled and reversed values, of lies made truths, that is the basic fabric of any war. And through it all occasionally breaks a bit of reality that no amount of self-delusion will make go away. And the news of Chuck's death was to me such a piece of this reality.

" . . . he took a direct hit in his glycol tank, and when I saw that white cloud blossom out behind him I knew he'd had it." It was Chuck's wing man speaking, a young Australian flying officer with whom Chuck had flown on all his missions. "We were over Abbeville that day—our target was the flak batteries that the goons had just moved up around that town—but the damndest thing . . . y'know, he must have known he was hit—he just had to—but instead of bailing out he put his nose down, and with the throttle wide open before the engine seized up, and with his guns firing, he crashed right into one of those gun sites. It's one of the damndest things I've ever seen! Why didn't he bail out? Why would a man do a thing like that?"

Why? I knew why. But I saw no sense in telling this young Australian about it . . . even trying to explain to him. "Thanks, Terry," I said, getting up and patting him on the shoulder, and leaving my unfinished drink on the bar, I walked out into the street. John followed me.

Three days later Michele found us. We had not moved out of London; in fact we had not moved out of our hotel room. For three days we did nothing but drink. We didn't eat, we didn't shave, we didn't do anything but drink. I would drink until I fell asleep, and then wake up and start drinking again. It was an insane, irrational thing I was doing and I knew it; but I just didn't want consciousness to seep into my brain, I didn't want to think, I didn't want to start dwelling on all the rotten things life can do to a man, and I didn't want any part of the bitterness and anger that seethed within me to come to the surface. I wanted to drown it, to keep it washed down in my soul where it belonged and where I could dissolve it with alcohol.

Michele, wise beyond her years about such matters, took one look at us, shuddered, and left, but an hour later she was back with an RCAF doctor she had shanghaied from the Air Ministry. The doctor quickly filled us with massive shots of vitamins and only he knew what else, and somehow he got us to a Turkish bath. Later that day, after Michele had gotten bowls of hot soup into us and allowed us one medicinal drink, we began to feel like human beings.

Chuck's death made me graphically aware of what the

odds were against me, and all the rest of us, and I didn't need a slide rule to figure them out. I have noticed that people engaged in a shooting war tend to build up an illusion of immunity. Chuck's death shattered this illusion for me.

From all this Michele and I seemed to grow closer together, it seemed to make us fully aware of how passing and tenuous our relationship was. I was spending all my leaves with her now, and they were quiet interludes that we spent alone in little country inns that she found. They were short idylls that we would spend together taking long walks in the country, or reading to each other, or just being quiet and enjoying the peace that two people who feel a tenderness for each other can share between them.

The summer passed, and then one morning in September we awakened to find that a security blackout had been clamped on our station. All leaves were cancelled, a patrolling guard unit was thrown around the perimeter of the airdrome, all phone calls, incoming and outgoing, were cut off, and no mail was allowed out. For the past two days we had been on a stand-down, which meant we were not assigned any operational duties, and ordinarily almost the entire squadron would have been granted passes. This time there had been no passes. Everyone was assigned some job to make certain that the squadron's fourteen Halifaxes were in top flying condition.

Rumors flew everywhere, and of course they grew wilder as the hours passed. The last time there had been any similar preparations and precautions was that summer when the RAF staged the first Thousand Raid on Hamburg—one thousand bombers over one target in one night. The raid had produced history's first man-made firestorm in which one hundred thousand living souls had been cremated. But even the precautions for that one had not been as elaborate as these.

At four o'clock that afternoon all air crew members were ordered over the tannoy system to report to the briefing room, and we knew that the suspenseful waiting was finally over and we would learn what the target was that had caused all this stir. After we were all seated the station commander and the squadron commander came in together, accompanied by the squadron intelligence officer who would do the briefing. Without wasting any words, this latter officer walked over to the map on the wall and pulled aside the screen that had been shielding it. The Danish town of Flensburg, right on the German border, was ringed with the red target crayon. Certainly no surprise here, for on several occasions during the past month the fjord outside Flensburg had been our target. It was known that the Germans had dug a huge submarine pen in this fjord. It was an important target, and a "hot" one because of the heavy concentration of flak batteries around it, but it scarcely seemed to warrant all the preparations that had been taking place.

" . . . most of you have been over this one before," the briefing officer continued, "and I hate to tell you, chaps, but to date our efforts have done exactly eff-all damage to this pen. It's still fully operational. So, this time we're going in low." A groan from the assembled group greeted this bit of news. "But you don't know yet how low," he added, a broad grin splitting his face. "I mean low . . . L–O–W. We're going in below the tops of that fjord. We're going to make our run in at rooftop height, we're going to follow that fjord right up its path, right to this sheer wall at the end"—he was now tracing with his pointer the route we were to take—"and then we dump our bomb load, balloon up over the face of the cliff, and get the hell out of there. We'll be using fused bombs, and they're set to go off five minutes after the last aircraft leaves the target. This will make you realize why the tight time schedule has to be watched closely."

I am certain every man present thought he was—or hoped he was—hearing incorrectly. This sensible man whom we all knew and with whom we had emptied many a bottle had said something about going in at rooftop height over one of the most heavily protected areas in occupied Europe. He had talked of flying into the face of a cliff . . . of "ballooning" up over the face of that cliff . . .

" . . . from the Danish underground, and from our own experience we know those banks are lined with flak batteries." Flipping a switch as he continued to talk, he threw the room into darkness, and then a blown-up aerial photo of the fjord was thrown onto the projecting screen. "Of course they can't traverse those guns below the horizontal . . . and even at the horizontal they would be firing into each other across the fjord, . . . so d'you see why we've got to go in low?"

The briefing officer was followed on the dais by several experts, and I got the impression that all these people were trying to make this operation sound like a sensible thing which sensible people might undertake. I still don't understand why the lot of us didn't rise to our feet, bow from the waist, politely say in unison, "Screw you, Jack," and walk out of the place. We just sat there like a lot of sheep, nodding our heads, and letting ourselves be persuaded that there might be some sort of future in this madness.

A civilian aerodynamics engineer from the Air Ministry in London had been brought down to give a lecture on the feasibility of "ballooning." He looked like a startled hare with his two large buck teeth peeping from beneath his bushy mustache. The diagrams he was drawing on the blackboard did make sense until I realized that after all I wouldn't be flying on that blackboard.

" . . . timing is the secret of this whole bit." It was the squadron engineering officer speaking now. "Everything has to be done at once. The bombardier has got to drop his bombs, the navigator has got to drop those flaps, full, and the pilot has got to hit those throttles wide open . . . and it's all got to be done at once. Everybody's got to act as one man. So . . . I'll be in the lead aircraft. Good luck, chaps."

Then we were addressed by the station commander. For

some moments he talked of the honor that had been accorded us in being selected for this delicate job, and then of the importance of this mission.

"In order that you will fully appreciate the importance of what we are asking you to do, a distinguished visitor from London has come down to speak with you." He drew himself to attention and barked out a command: "Room! AT-TENTION!"

We all jumped to our feet and came to attention as the air police officer standing by the door threw it open. And into the room walked, or rather shuffled, an unmistakable figure wearing an ill-fitting uniform of an air commodore in the Royal Air Force. Winston Churchill walked slowly, deliberately to the dais, and then, waving his hand, said, "Thank you, gentlemen . . . be seated, please."

I don't know how long he talked to us, for that genius of the spoken word had the ability to make time stand still. First he spoke of the absolute necessity of destroying that submarine pen, and he knew the exact amount of ship's tonnage those submarines had sunk during the past three months. He graphically broke down what that tonnage represented in units of war material, and then he spoke to us of ourselves. And his words somehow made us remember our dreams, our hopes, and our ideals, and he made these ideals seem more worthwhile than ever. He rekindled within each of us that spark which is in all men, that spark which fanned to life can raise even the most self-centered above and beyond himself. With his words he enlarged each one of us to the fullest image of ourselves, and he made us feel that at that moment the eyes of history and all posterity were upon us. He likened war to a game of chess in which each piece became the most important one on the board when it was that piece's turn to move—and now it was our turn. He spoke simply and directly, without recourse to any tricks of oratory and without stooping to any histrionics—he seemed to be purposely underplaying his case—and when he finished there was not a man in that room who had not been moved to the core of his being. This was a hard-bitten squadron of veterans, and yet I know every man in that room felt the same sensation in his spine that I felt in mine.

He spoke then of how this entire operation had been explained to him, of how he realized what had been asked of us, and how we all realized, of course, that only unhesitating boldness would carry this day. He paused then and looked out at all of us, and an impish grin began to form on his expressive, rubbery features.

"I think I should remind you chaps," he said slowly, "of an old English proverb . . . one I first heard as a wee tot at my nanny's knee—'Faint heart never fucked a spider.' "

The English may have the reputation of being a cold and unemotional race, but the roar that came from the throats of us all as we jumped spontaneously to our feet almost tore the roof off the building. Needless to say, within a few hours that submarine pen had been blown to hell. But when it was all over and I had quieted my nerves with a slug of the ever-comforting brandy, I was just as glad I had been facing backward in the rear turret and did not have to sit up front and watch the wall of that fjord rush at me. "Ballooning" tactics? Well, old scared-hare and his blackboard were right. They worked.

13.

When one has flown combat missions for any
length of time, memory blends them together
until they become all of a piece. The one other raid that
stands out clearly from the rest was my last one—and it was
by accident that I even took part in that mission. I had not
been scheduled to fly that night but was standing at the end
of the runway with the operations officers as he, with his
Aldis lamp, signaled the aircraft and got them airborne, one
following right on the tail of the other. The third-from-last
Halifax was standing poised, waiting for the "go" flick of the
light when suddenly the pilot signaled us. In a dogtrot we
hurried over to see what the trouble was, and the pilot, with
a frantically jabbing finger was motioning us toward the rear
turret. During the past two weeks we had taken more than
our usual share of casualties, and this was one of the green
crews that had been sent us from the replacement depot. In
fact this was the first combat mission for this crew. Running

around to the rear turret and motioning with my hand because of the wash of the props and the tinny roar of the engines, I got the gunner to understand I wanted him to swing the turret around and open the door.

"What's the problem?" I bellowed at him over the noise.

The gunner, a huge farm boy from Yorkshire, held out his hand; and there, nestling in the great palm, were the remains of what had once been a finely adjusted gun sight.

"It coom apart in me 'and!" he shouted in his Yorkshire accent. It was as though a bear had got hold of a fine, jeweled Swiss watch.

"Get the bloody hell out of there!" I roared at him, and as he extricated his lumbering bulk from the turret, I snatched off his parachute harness and buckled it on myself over my best uniform. That plane had to go on the mission, and there had better be someone in the turret who could hit a target without the aid of a gunsight. Perhaps I could do something with the help of the tracers.

As we got airborne and headed out across the Channel, the realization of how stupid I had just been crashed into my mind—and it was that parachute harness which acted as the catalyst. For some reason known only to himself the plowboy had been wearing an unneeded sheepskin-lined leather flying jacket, and the harness had been adjusted to all that bulk. There was now enough slack in the harness to hang a horse, and it was all hanging down between my legs. If I had to bail out and the parachute opened, that slack would snap taut right into my crotch! With this sickening picture in mind I reached behind me for the adjusting buckles, but in the cramped quarters I couldn't do anything with them, so I pulled the slack up around my chest and offered a small prayer. By now I was beginning to feel that I had used up all my luck; but maybe it would hold for one more time.

For an hour or more we droned along uneventfully. We had not run into any heavy concentrations of flak, and mi-

raculously no night fighters had challenged us. The target
this night was Dusseldorf, and Intelligence had assured us
the flak would be light. Suddenly a cold thought entered my
mind: for the past half-hour I had not noticed any other
bombers flying in our direction and this despite the fact we
should have been right in the middle of the bomber stream.
Slowly I swung the turret in its full arc—nothing out there
but an occasional fleecy patch of white cloud, shimmering in
the bright moonlight. And then I looked down at the ground
eight thousand feet below us. Oh, no! But blinking my eyes
wouldn't make it go away. The *Kölner Dom!* The majestic
twin spires of the Cologne Cathedral were pointing into the
sky at me. The bulk of the old Gothic edifice was bathed in
moonlight, and the moonlight was shimmering from the
waters of the river as it made its unmistakable bend around
the church. There we were, right on top of Cologne . . .
alone.

The pilot must have instinctively sensed that something
was wrong, for I heard a microphone click on, and then his
voice crackled in the earphones. "Hullo, navigator! . . .
Where are we?"

For what seemed interminable seconds there was dead
silence, and then the well-bred, English-public-school accents
of the navigator came over the intercom, "I'm fucked if I
know, old boy."

The groan of despair did not even have time to escape
my lips before everything seemed to begin happening at
once. The eerie purple light of the radio-controlled searchlight, the master searchlight of the Cologne air defense system locked onto us, and having seen this happen to other
bombers, I knew there would be no escaping it. No maneuvering, no "jinking," no diving nor turning nor any amount
of speed would shake off that relentless finger. With the
range signaled to them from this automatic light the entire
searchlight complex now locked onto us and we were "coned,"
the most dreaded thing that could happen to any bomber

crew. The sky around us and the aircraft itself were lighted up like Broadway on New Year's Eve, and then it came. The German gunners had a sitting duck for a target, and all they had to do was pour their fire up into the apex of that cone, and there was no way for them to miss. In the bright, blinding light there was no flashing coming from the flak bursts now, but suddenly our whole piece of illuminated sky filled with brown, oily puffs of smoke. Pieces of shrapnel began hitting us, and it sounded like wet gravel being hurled against sheet metal. Then we started taking direct hits, and the aircraft jumped and bucked and thrashed, and pieces of it were being blown off, and I could see them whipping past me. Then the fire started, and I could smell it and see the long tongues of flame streaming out from the wings. The intercom was now dead and so was the hydraulic system that operated the turret, but with the manual crank I quickly turned the turret around, opened the doors, and was preparing to push myself backwards out into the sky when a burst of light, fine shrapnel sprinkled my whole back. It felt as though the points of a dozen white hot pokers had suddenly jabbed into me. My one prayer at that moment was that the flak had not cut the parachute harness draped over my back. The parachute harness! Oh, God . . . get that slack out of your crotch! I dropped, clutching the slack around my midriff with my left hand, and pulled the rip cord on my chest pack with my right. I was now conscious of the dead silence through which I was falling. Gone was the aircraft with its roaring engines and miraculously the flak had stopped. But one searchlight glued itself onto me and began following me downward. Then the chute opened, and my fall was suddenly, jarringly halted, and I bobbed upward like a yo-yo in the hand of some idiot giant. With a tearing, rending noise the slack snapped taut around my chest, and I felt my whole rib cage cave in. Then I passed out.

I was jarred out of it by the thudding impact as my body hit the ground and then by a sharp pain in my left hip. My flask! I suddenly recalled the flask of brandy I now carried at all times in my hip pocket.

A German sergeant, a *Feldwebel,* and four privates appeared. They had been assigned to follow my descent in the glare of the single searchlight that had picked me up. In view of my intentions toward them and all their fellows just a few minutes previously I wasn't sure just what sort of reception I was going to receive, but I never expected the good-humored curiosity with which they greeted me. I made an effort to rise to my feet but soon gave that up as a hopeless cause and lay back down, waiting for whatever was going to happen. One of the privates kneeled down beside me and, fingering my uninflated, yellow Mae West under the parachute harness, said with a big grin on his face, *"Schwimmblase, ja?"*

The sergeant, pushing the private out of the way, quickly searched me for weapons and then emptied my pockets and removed the dog tag from around my neck. He was holding the half-empty pack of cigarettes he had extracted from my pocket, and I pointed to this and numbled something about liking a cigarette before I died. As he put one in my mouth and lighted it for me, I motioned for him to have one and pass them to his men. After looking around to make sure no officer was approaching, they all lighted up and dragged appreciatively on the Virginia tobacco. Then the sergeant with a big grin on his face made the statement I was to hear frequently from the Germans, a statement they always made with a somewhat wistful tone, "For you dcr var is ofer!"

I tried to get to my feet and found that I was numb from the waist down, and I began to fear that it wasn't just the war that was over for me.

"Ach, so," the sergeant said, "ve get a litter."

After a few minutes one of the soldiers returned with a stretcher and rolled me onto it. With a lot of good natured chattering they carried me some two hundred yards across the fields to what was apparently the command post of the

Cologne defense batteries. There were numerous cars and lorries parked around the large wooden shack that was the office; motorcycles were driving up and departing, and no one paid any attention to me as my escort set the stretcher down near the doorway. The sergeant went into the office carrying my dog tag and my meager personal belongings, but he was back in a few minutes and stood beside the stretcher looking down at me. "So, *Engländer* . . . der Herr Major vants to see you."

By some act of will power I got myself to my feet. I'm not sure just how I managed this, but I thought that tradition called for me to face this moment with dignity. I must have been a ridiculous sight as I marched into that office. The sergeant followed along closely behind—I'm sure he expected me to fall flat on my face.

The Luftwaffe major seated behind the flat-topped desk did not bother to look up as I entered but continued to turn my dog tag, over and over. In a moment or two, still not bothering to look up, he bellowed out a string of commands to the sergeant, and this poor man, snapping to attention, shouted, *"Jawohl, Herr Major!"* and almost tore down the door in his haste to obey. In a minute there was a timid knock on the door, and an orderly with a bad case of sniffles and carrying a shoeshine kit entered the office. Leaning back in his chair and throwing one black-booted leg up onto the desk, the major motioned for the orderly to start shining the already glistening riding boot. He still had not looked at me.

Suddenly, without warning, the major leaped to his feet, kicked the shoeshine box across the office and started screaming at the terrified orderly, who, with the major's shouts of *"Raus! Raus!"* ringing in his ears, tore out the door. Now that this major was standing up I could understand some of the terror the orderly had shown, for this was a formidable-looking man: he was at least six feet four inches tall, and he was big and broad without any fat showing. Such a blond,

Teutonic specimen as this must have warmed the hearts of Herr Hitler and his toady Dr. Rosenberg, for he almost lent credence to their theory of the superiority of the "pure Aryan."

After the orderly had slammed the door shut behind him, the major turned around to me and, with his hands on his hips, stood looking directly at me for the first time since I had entered. Slowly a grin began spreading across his bony features.

"How's that, Mr. Harsh?" he asked in perfect English, without a trace of accent. "Is that the way a Hun's supposed to act? That's the trouble with you bloody English . . . you think all us Germans are Huns. Now sit down—before you fall down—and I'll get a medic in here to you."

The remainder of that night is mostly a blur in my memory. I remember the major pulling a bottle of cognac from his desk drawer and pouring me several generous slugs of this as a medic administered first aid to me; I remember a pain-filled ride in a car through the dark, rubbled streets of Cologne; I remember being admitted to a large hospital in that city; and I remember the glaring lights of an operating room. But for some reason, beyond all else, I remember the neatly framed posed pictures of Hitler hanging from the walls of all the offices into which I was led.

Two days later I emerged from a morphine-induced coma lying in a hospital cot. I was swathed in tapes and bandages. For two weeks I was kept in the Cologne hospital, and not much of that stay remains in my mind other than the great kindness and mercy that was shown me by the Catholic sisters who ran the hospital. If at this late date it is of any worth to those sisters, I would like them to know that because of them one man gained the sure awareness that kindness and mercy and compassion require far greater inner strength than the military-inspired attitudes of belligerency, self-sufficiency, and toughness. Sophisticated savagery can be taught. Gentleness springs from the human heart.

Almost nightly during my stay in the Cologne hospital the airraid sirens would sound, and the patients, both civilians and military, would be shepherded down into the basement to the airraid shelters. When this occurred on my first night the doctor in charge of the ward, a Nazi colonel in the medical corps, came to the door of the ward and bellowed out the evacuation order. As I struggled up to a sitting position and got my legs over the side of the bed he strode halfway down the aisle and stood glaring at me.

"Not you, *Engländer!*" he shouted. "Those are your *Kameraden* up there . . . you lie here, and let them drop their bombs on you—as they do on our women and children!"

I lay there alone and listened as the bombs began whistling down and krumping and shaking the hospital and rattling the windows. One of the sisters slipped back into the ward, and sitting down on the side of my cot, she reached for my hand.

"We stay together," she announced, and then added tentatively, "Maybe we pray together, no?"

Nothing I could say, no pleading on my part, would get her to leave and go below to shelter, and from then on for the rest of my stay in the hospital she would come and sit on the side of my bed, and we would hold hands during the air raids. I think she must have sensed that I put but small stock in prayer as such, and so, while we wasted no time in prayer or in the telling of beads, we spent much time in talking of matters of the human heart and the human spirit. I think her initial disappointment in me when she discovered that I was not a "God-fearing Christian" was somewhat alleviated when she discovered that I believed implicitly in Jesus Christ the man.

By now the air raids on Cologne were an almost nightly occurrence, and on those nights when the city was not the target of a full-scale raid, the RAF would send over a single, highflying Mosquito to drop one stick of bombs, just to assure the people of the city that they had not been forgotten. Every night we would sit together and talk, and as a stick of bombs began its relentless fall toward us and as the explosions got louder and nearer, the clasp of our hands grew tighter.

After two weeks in the Cologne hospital I was transferred to Dulag Luft, the Luftwaffe interrogation center outside of Frankfurt-am-Main. My torso was still taped up like an Egyptian mummy, and I was still very weak. The authorities must have realized that escape was out of the question for me; at least that is the only reason I can think of for their sending me off accompanied by a lone guard. His name was Adolf, and if Hitler could have seen this namesake of his, he would have given up the war as a hopeless cause. I suppose every army, in the natural course of things, produces its own version of Sad Sack, but Adolf was a travesty even of caricature; his tunic was too small for him, and his bony wrists hung out four inches below his cuffs, his trousers were too large, and one had the impression he took two steps before those trousers moved at all. His feet were actually mates, but his boots were not. The left one was several sizes too small for him, while the right one was too big. Accordingly he walked by hobbling pigeon-toed on his left foot, while dragging his right. His steel helmet kept slipping down over his eyes. To have his vision suddenly cut off in this manner never ceased to startle him, and he would quickly push the coal scuttle back on his head and peep out at the world with apprehensive eyes.

The train trip, even under wartime conditions, should have taken not more than a few hours, but with Adolf as a cicerone the trip took two days. At the very outset he got us on the wrong train, and we had gone twenty miles in the wrong direction before the train crew discovered our mistake and put us off at a way station, where we had to wait several hours for a train going back to our starting point and then begin the journey all over again.

To give him some semblance of a warrior, someone had strapped a Luger in a huge wooden holster around his waist. This heavy weapon caused him no end of embarrassment, for he had not the foggiest notion as to what he was expected to do with it. When we got back to the Cologne railway station after our abortive start, Adolf was suddenly stricken with an urgent and unpostponable peristaltic twitch. Going into the barnlike washroom and walking up to the row of doored cubicles, Adolf unbuckled the gun belt, took off his tunic, and handed the lot to me. The washroom was aswarm with German troops in full battle gear, SS men in their black uniforms were everywhere; and there I stood in the heart of the Cologne railway station in a torn and blood-stained uniform of a flight lieutenant in the Royal Air Force with a huge loaded Luger in my hand. And Adolf thought *he* had to shit.

On leaving the hospital we had been given a small box lunch of black bread and sausage, which was to sustain us during the short trip; but due to our meanderings our meager larder was depleted long before we arrived at our destination. But experience has taught me that often within the depths of those whom the world may carelessly dismiss as fools lies a certain craftiness which will pull them through trials which would baffle those cut from more conventional material. Every railway station where we were forced to stop and wait for trains was filled with combat troops, many of them on leave from the Russian front, and I had noticed the puzzled looks on their weather-beaten faces when they had seen me and tried to figure out just what or who I might be. At that, I must have presented a weird sight, dressed in a blood-stained blue uniform, with wings sewn to the chest of my tunic and with a strange-looking crowned badge on my cap. Adolf too had undoubtedly noticed these puzzled glances, and as we began to get hungry he capitalized on the situation. Circulating among the waiting troops, he let it be known that he had in tow a real, live, breathing, captured

Englischerflieger, and because one of the hallmarks of any combat veteran is a more-or-less good-humored curiosity about his enemy, I soon became the center of a knot of troops wherever we stopped. Also I have yet to see any European who is not eager to try out his schoolboy English at any opportunity. I soon got over the feeling of being an animal in a zoo when these troops began sharing their travel rations of cheese (put up in metal tubes, like toothpaste), their sausages, and their black bread with Adolf and me. The zoo feeling left me entirely when they began breaking out flasks of *Schnaps,* and before the trip was over I had learned the chorus of the *Horst Wessel* by heart.

14.

Dulag Luft was a reception center maintained by the Luftwaffe where all newly captured Allied fliers were detained for varying periods and where information was extracted from them by the use of shrewd psychological methods. Such was the high state of British Intelligence that not a single British airman was ever captured who did not have a complete picture in his mind of exactly what was going to happen to him during his detention in Dulag Luft. All air crews were constantly given lectures on this subject, and while these lectures were always prefaced by the honeyed words, "This is just in case you chaps have the bad luck to come down on the other side . . . ," they were amazingly accurate descriptions of the Germans' methods of obtaining information. In addition to the lectures we were also shown professionally made motion pictures, so that when we arrived at Dulag, we were somewhat like actors stepping into roles for which we had been well-coached. The lines for our roles were easily remembered: "Name, rank, and number only."

Of course all of us realized that should the Gestapo want to extract information from us they would bloody well get the information—and no amount of chest-beating heroics would alter this fact. But Intelligence had assured us that Dulag was under the direction of the Luftwaffe and that between Goering's Luftwaffe and Himmler's Gestapo there existed a professional jealousy that bordered on ill-feeling. The Luftwaffe would do its utmost to keep all captured airmen under its jurisdiction, and within reasonable limits we could expect to be treated according to the Geneva Convention.

So, on entering the gate of the compound, I knew exactly what was in store for me. First, I was given a hot shower, and my dressings and tapings were changed by a medic. Then I was put into a small, wooden detention cell, bare of any furniture other than a cot, and I was left there alone, naked, for three days. Twice a day a guard would unlock the door and hand me a slop bucket, a plate of cabbage soup, and a chunk of black bread; he would never say a word to me. I soon realized he was under strict orders not to speak to me, and as one means of passing the time I began playing a game with him. Whenever the guard opened the door I would deliver long speeches in my schoolboy German, as though speaking to myself—speeches I had spent the whole day thinking up—and they were usually on the same theme: "It is rumored that Hitler's mother had fleas," or "It is rumored that the neighbors saved their soup bones for Hitler's mother," or "It is rumored in certain parts of Austria that Hitler's mother used to run out from under the front porch and bite the postman in the leg."

Certainly it was childish and idiotic, but it was a great pastime, and it helped me brush up on my execrable German. At least I knew my German was understandable: the back of the guard's neck would turn a fiery red whenever

I would deliver one of my soliloquies. Should I ever see that guard again, I would like to thank him for helping me retain whatever tattered shreds of sanity I may possess today.

After three days the questioning began. A Luftwaffe captain, a *Hauptmann,* entered my cell, sat down on the end of the cot, gave me a cigarette, and began chatting amiably. He was Charley Charming himself with a mouthful of teeth like Chiclets, and he exuded charm and comradery from every pore. He explained he was a fighter pilot who had been wounded on the Russian front, and that the Russians were subhuman animals against whom we, the British, should also be fighting, and that what a shame our two great countries could not settle their differences as gentlemen should. He knew, of course, that Germany could not win this war, and he had taken the precaution of sending his wife and children to South America, where he hoped to join them after the war, and on and on.

Intelligence had prepared us for just this sort of thing, and I sat there repeating over and over, like a broken, crazy record, "Name, rank, and serial number . . . name, rank, and serial number . . . name, rank, and . . ."

After several days of this charade Charley Charming gave up. One morning a helmeted guard came for me and said, *"Kommen Sie mit,"* an expression that was to be the prelude to so many happenings in my life for the next three years. The guard marched me down a long, echoing corridor, through an office filled with girls working at desks, and into another large office where six Luftwaffe officers were waiting for me at a long table. The guard marched me to the center of the room and barked "Halt!" and there I stood naked as a jaybird. I am sure I was still a bright scarlet from having been paraded without a stitch on through that roomful of women; but standing at attention in my bare feet, I did my best to look like a dignified British officer.

For over an hour they shot questions at me, and the girl stenographer who had entered the room kept shorthand

notes of the proceedings. It was obvious what they were
after: they wanted information about the radar the British
had now developed. The British were now bombing, ac-
curately, through ten-tenths cloud, and it was apparent that
this was not being achieved through luck. Some device was
being used, and they had to know what it was. But they were
wasting their time questioning any members of captured air
crews, for none of us, purposely, knew anything about it,
and even Gestapo torture could not extract from a man information he did not possess. The only thing any of us knew
about radar was that it was referred to as "the box of tricks";
any of us, that is, except the navigators, and all they knew
was that over the target they were to turn a knob on a black
box and that suddenly the target would appear on the screen
right through a dense cloud cover. Magic, that's what it was.
"What's the German word for *magic?*"

After two days of this the board of officers gave up on
me; they were either as sick as I was of hearing my broken
record, or they surmised correctly that I knew nothing about
radar. But whatever the reason, Charley Charming appeared
in my cell one morning, and he had all my clothing with
him.

"I apologize for the inconvenience the delay in our hotel's cleaning service has caused you," he said with a grin.
"I'm afraid our service is suffering from the war conditions.
But seriously. I had one of the girls clean up your uniform a
bit, and she stitched up some of the rents. And because
winter is coming and you'll need it I've brought you an overcoat." As he said this he held up an ankle-length, flowing
khaki overcoat. "Is it not beautiful? It's a Polish cavalry
officer's greatcoat. I envy you the wearing of it. But as your
friends the *Juden* say, 'Wear it in health!' "

"Put your clothing on," Charley Charming said after I
had finished admiring my new greatcoat. "I want for you to
see something."

Leading me back through the room filled with women—

the German equivalent of the WAAF—he led me into another large room, lined with steel filing cabinets.

"Let me see now," he said pausing at the door, "Bomber Command . . . Four Group." Then going over to one of the cabinets and pulling out a drawer, he added, "Ach, so, here we are . . . 102 Squadron. You see, we know the code letters on your Halifax that we shot down." From a bulging manila folder he extracted several single-typed sheets of paper. "*Ja* . . . here we are. Group Captain Sanders, station commander . . . Wing Commander Duckworth, squadron commander. Now then, let's see . . . you were in B Flight . . . Flight Lieutenant Gaskell, flight commander. And look at this, Mr. Harsh . . . my, my . . . Flight Lieutenant Harsh, squadron gunnery officer. Isn't that amazing! H-m . . . and it says here you are an American, Mr. Harsh. Why did you not transfer to the American Air Force?"

Although a few minutes before I had actually been naked, I had not then felt as naked as I did now.

"*Ja, ja,* I know . . . 'Name, rank, and number' . . . h-m, and it says here on September fifth the Duke of Kent visited your squadron. Was it a good luncheon you turned on for him in the officers' mess, Mr. Harsh?"

Dropping the folder back in the file, he slammed it shut with a bang. " 'Name, rank, and number' . . . bah! Who needs it?"

After a long, gruesome train journey on the hard wooden benches of a third-class European day coach, I and two other RAF officers were finally delivered to the Luftwaffe prison camp, Stalag Luft III, located in a pine forest near the town of Sagan, in Silesia. This time the three guards who accompanied us were not Adolfs but were *Unteroffiziere* who knew their business. With them guarding us, even the idea of escape seemed ridiculous, so I gave up the idea and concentrated on trying to make myself as comfortable as possible.

Stalag Luft III was a sprawling complex of barbed-wire fences enclosing wooden one-story barracks. The whole camp was divided into compounds holding one thousand Allied air force officers for easier control by the Germans. The new North Compound had just been completed, and it was into this I was to be herded. My two young English traveling companions were to be sent to the East Compound.

First I was taken to the German command center, or *Vorlager,* where I was photographed in rogues-gallery style. A minute description was made of me for the records, and I was issued a new dog tag, a metal oblong with my number on it . . . *Kriegsgefangener* #10522.

After this routine I was escorted over to the large, double gates of the North Compound by a Luftwaffe *Feldwebel* . . . my first encounter with Sergeant Major Glemnitz.

Through the high strands of the barbed wire I could see the prisoners, dressed in odd bits and pieces of RAF uniforms, walking about in the camp or standing in groups talking and apparently paying no attention to this new arrival. As soon as the gate was slammed shut and locked behind me, three officers in threadbare uniforms walked up to me as though they had been expecting me. One wore the three stripes of a wing commander on his sleeves, one the two-and-a-half stripes of a squadron leader, and the other the two stripes of a flight lieutenant.

" 'Morning, old boy," said the wing commander. "Would you come with us, please?"

They escorted me into one of the barracks and into a room lined with double-deck wooden bunks. The bunks, a long crude wooden table, eight straight chairs, and a coal-burning stove over in a corner were the room's only furniture.

"This is just routine, old boy," said the wing commander. "We have to make sure the Hun isn't trying to put a 'plant' in here on us . . ."

After a few minutes grilling by the three, my identity had been established, and they were satisfied that I was a bona fide RAF officer and was actually who I claimed to be.

The two other officers left us alone after the wing commander said that he would like to talk to me for a moment before taking me over to the room to which I had been assigned. For a long moment he looked at me silently, speculatively. Then dropping his voice, he said. "You know, Harsh, of course, that you're checked out with Intelligence?"

"Yes, sir."

"And you know what to do?"

"Yes, sir."

"Very well. In a day or so *Hauptmann* Pieber, the German *Lageroffizier,* will bring in to you the letter form the Huns supply us and on which once a month we are allowed to write home. When you put the day's date on the top of the letter I will let you know what the code word is for that particular date . . . and I will let you know what message to code into your letter. Understood?"

"Yes, sir."

"H-m . . . by the tone of your voice I don't think you really quite understand. The daily code word puzzles you? Quite. Well, we get it every night on the wireless we have hidden here in the camp. It—and other things—are coded into the midnight news broadcast from London over the BBC. The wireless we have hidden was brought in by a paratroop major who was captured at Dunkirk . . . he brought it in in a soccer ball . . . the bloody Huns never thought to search a soccer ball. And that's how we knew you were on your way here. They let us know the names of all mail contacts. Intelligence knew you were captured almost as soon as you did."

British Intelligence, I was beginning to think, probably knew what Hitler had for breakfast that morning.

"Oh, yes . . . there's one other thing before I show you to the room you'll share with seven others . . . Collett will want to see you. He's the wallah who keeps up on travel conditions here in Germany . . . sort of our travel agent . . . just in case one of us might like to take a trip."

Collett turned out to be a ruddy-faced, beefy New Zealand squadron leader with a huge flowing mustache which he kept stroking back to his ears.

"Tell me everything you saw out there," he began after the wing commander had introduced us. "What the trains were like, the stations, what sort of passes your guard had to show . . . don't skip anything you can remember . . . no detail."

As I talked, trying to recall everything that happened on my recent train journey, he took notes on a small piece of paper—chewable size—that he held in his hand.

"Very good, old boy," he said after he had pumped me dry. "By putting all these bits and pieces together, we can keep a fairly accurate picture of what it's like out there . . . should one of us get out. Now that I've picked your brains, you probably have a lot of questions you'd like to ask about this place. Fire away."

Food. Naturally the matter of food had been the one thing uppermost in my mind whenever I contemplated the conditions under which I would have to serve out an indeterminate number of years.

"That part of it's not really too bad," he said thoughtfully. "But you've got to remember this is wartime Germany. From the Germans we get a small daily issue of black bread and either a few potatoes or a cup of sauerkraut. Then once a week they give us a small sausage ration, about a tablespoon of jam, and an equal amount of ersatz butter or fat. It's bloody little, but on top of this, once a week every man is issued a package of food that comes from the International Red Cross in Switzerland. God bless the Red Cross . . . and so says every man who's a prisoner . . . for without 'em we'd be in damn sorry shape, that I can tell you."

After listing the items of food in a Red Cross parcel—a tin of bully beef, a small tin of butter, a carton of sugar, a package of raisins or prunes, a tin of dried milk, a pack of tea or coffee, a bar of chocolate, and a pack of cigarettes—he went on to tell me of the administration of the camp and of the routine that had been established to ensure the greatest good for the greatest number.

"You'll share a room with seven other officers, and because it's been proved to be the best way, your food parcel will go into the common larder. Your mess will consist of the eight of you. Of course the whole camp is under tight military discipline. Wing Commander Day—he's the one who just brought you over here—is the senior British officer —the SBO—and he appoints those administrative officers needed to keep things from falling into chaos. Other than that you're free to do as you damn' please in here. We do get a limited number of books—again through the Red Cross—we have an educational officer who has set up a schedule of regular classes covering almost any subject—this is an excellent place to learn any language—and so, all in all, we get by and stay reasonably sane. And, oh, yes . . . there is an 'X Organization'—but you'll learn about that later."

Saying this, he stood up and held out his hand. "Good luck, old boy . . . and someday soon we'll have a drink together in Odinino's in London."

I was feeling pretty rocky from my stay in the hospital, and I fell into the hard wooden bunk that someone pointed out, closed my eyes, and tried to assimilate all I had been through and had heard this day. I was still weak, my whole rib cage ached under the adhesive tape that was by now beginning to itch maddeningly, and a whole covey of frightened birds was fluttering around in my empty stomach. For the first time I was beginning to wonder why I had bothered to pull the rip cord on that parachute; but of one thing I was sure—just then I would have given whatever there was left of my soul for a hot cup of tea or coffee.

As if in answer to what I had not realized had been a prayer, a voice from the bunk above me said, "In one hour we'll have our midday snack . . . d'you think you can hold on that long?"

Opening my eyes, I looked up and there hanging over the side of the upper bunk, upside down, was a face peering at me. It had blue eyes with long lashes, inordinately long lashes for a man. The whole face had the expression of being quite amazed at whatever it beheld. This was my first sight of John Agrell, and after I got to know him I came to realize that nothing on the top side of this earth would ever amaze John Agrell—he had seen it all.

"It's not much of a snack," he added. "A cup of tea, a hard British biscuit, and a bit of bully beef . . . but it'll keep your soul within your body . . . providing your soul doesn't require too much."

He swung around and dropped himself out of his bunk onto the floor beside me. There was nothing quiet about that drop of his, for on his feet he was wearing a pair of huge Dutch wooden shoes, and when he hit the floor the whole room shook.

"This, my friend, is an ill-omened day for you," he said, grinning down at me. "You will observe that you are occupying the only empty bunk in this room. By our fellow inmates this is considered the least desirable bunk in all of Germany—because it is beneath me. You see, my friend, I not only snore at night . . . but also I break wind. However, to compensate for these negative qualities—these nocturnal rumblings, both fore and aft—I would have you know I am chaste, pure of heart, and an intrepid slayer of dragons. My name, sir, is John Agrell—your obedient servant."

Surely high up on the list of traumatic human experiences is that of being taken prisoner—any kind of prisoner. We all live by our illusions, and one of the greatest of all these illusions is the one that we are really free; rob us of that myth and there is no solace to be found. But of all prisoners, perhaps the prisoner of war finds it hardest to adjust, for suddenly, usually right out of the heat of battle, he finds himself at the complete mercy of those whom just a few minutes before he was trying to kill and who were trying to kill him. I was now defenseless and completely at the mercy of my enemies: in Shakespeare's words, "naked before mine enemies."

However, it would be a safe wager that of the thousand prisoners in the North Compound of Stalag Luft III, I was the only ex-convict, and so, for me, the psychological adjustment was basically a minor one. I had been through all this before. I don't believe I had fully made the adjustment to once more being "free" when I found myself again imprisoned. It was almost as though I had traded one set of guards in black Stetsons for another set in steel helmets. And while they may have spoken different languages, the jobs for which they were being paid had the same end in view. But the irony of my predicament placed me in an ambivalent position that could not be shared by any of my fellow war prisoners; if the gods considered this a joke I took a bloody pale view of their sense of humor!

Very quickly I settled into the routine of my new life. Once more I fell back on the trick I had learned on the chain gang: of living one day at a time. In the back of my mind was the sure knowledge that someday the war would end (if from nothing else but sheer exhaustion on the part of both sides) and that if the Germans won I would probably end up in the salt mines of Poland, if the Allies won . . . well, I would once more have to cope with the task of learning to live in a "normal" world. In the meantime . . . "When do we eat?"

Looking back on some trying period in our lives, we tend to forget the unpleasant, the harrowing, and the downright frightful aspects and remember instead the pleasant moments, the comical interludes, and the other leavenings that made the horror bearable. As the years pass I tend to forget the ever-present menace of the Gestapo; my memory glides over those soul-chilling moments when the Gestapo and the SS would come in and search the camp, those awful moments when the Gestapo would threaten to line us up and shoot every tenth man until we surrendered the radio they were sure we had hidden, or the utterly helpless and hopeless time, toward the end of the war, when Count Folke Bernadotte of Sweden, as a representative of the International Red Cross, was allowed into the camp and slipped word to us that Hitler had ordered Himmler to have every one of us shot rather than let us be liberated by the approaching Russians. The human mind offers a merciful buffering against the remembrance of such moments and brings to the fore those memories that one can cherish and that bring warmth to the soul.

I will always remember the great kindness of my mess mates during the difficult first few months of my captivity. When I arrived I had nothing except the clothes I stood up in, but most of these men had been in the camp long enough to have acquired at least some of the "needments" of living. Every six months one's relatives at home, through the auspices of the Red Cross, could send off a prisoner-of-war package, and such was the efficiency of this organization that at least eighty per cent of these packages eventually reached the addressee. Those who had received these parcels were able to share their bounty with those of us who had not yet received our own. In this way I received a toothbrush from one of my mess mates, a tube of toothpaste from another, a razor and two blades (the blades would have to last me four months), and from yet another—glorious day!—a woolen hand-knit extra sweater he happened to have. All these necessities were presented freely, in an offhand manner and with no thought of recompense; they were simply repayment for the kindness and consideration the donor had received when he had first arrived and had himself been in need of such things. During my years in that camp I never saw this cyclic demonstration of brotherhood and selfless help broken.

John Agrell was a most fortunate prisoner—he had friends in Sweden. During World War II the Germans were most proper in their dealings with the Swedes, for they were getting the entire output of Swedish steel—and without having to occupy the country, which would have pinned down many divisions of troops needed elsewhere. In fairness to the Swedes, their hands were tied in this matter, for it was either produce or face the horror of Nazi occupation; so, they quietly produced the minimum amount of steel they could get by with. The Germans, not wanting to upset this delicate balance, were meticulous in their dealings with this neutral country. Any parcel coming from Sweden addressed to a prisoner of war was sped along by the Germans. In this way, at least once a month, John would receive one of these parcels from his friends. They usually contained food: heaven-sent tins of butter, cheese, biscuits, tea, and jam, and all these things John turned in to the common larder of our mess.

As priceless as these things were, even more important to us were the books. Every package contained at least two Penguin English edition books, well-printed in paperback form. Also John's friends would send him any book he might want, just for the asking, and in two weeks time we would receive it. I say we for, bunking directly under John, I had first chance at this El Dorado of literature. Then the books would be circulated around the camp until they were so frayed and worn as to be no longer legible. I now had the chance to read every book I had ever wanted to read, books I had always promised myself I would someday read, and I settled in to enjoy to the fullest this rare opportunity. Under these circumstances I was convinced I could sit out the war, no matter how long it lasted. It was just as well that at that time I did not know of another little joke the gods had in store for me.

15.

One of the lessons I learned from war is that very often it is your friends who will get you killed; you don't have to worry too much about your enemy —you know only too well what his intentions are. But beware of your friends!

I had been in that camp less than two weeks before John Agrell made me a marked man with the Germans and got me thrown into the cooler for ten days on bread and water. Ever since my arrival I had noticed that John, sitting cross-legged on his upper bunk, had been working like a determined beaver on bits and pieces of old RAF uniforms that he had got hold of. He had worked loose two boards beside his bunk in the partition that separated our room from the one next door and in this, which he called his hidey-hole, he kept the uniform, his needle and thread, and the pieces of chalk he had scrounged from the educational officer. Once he was sure the camp was free of ferrets—the special German guards who patrolled inside the camp—he would open up his hidey-hole and start working on the uniform with feverish intensity. He would work until one of his friends, watching the gate, would signal him that a ferret was re-entering the compound, and he would then quickly return the uniform to its hiding place and resume his reading.

"I can tell by the expression on your face that you're practically popping with curiosity as to what I'm doing," he said one day. "But you're too polite to ask . . . so, I'll tell you. I, friend Harsh, am making a German *Feldwebel*'s uniform, and in this uniform I'm going to walk out of that gate. And as repayment for the distasteful fate of having to sleep beneath me I'm going to take you with me."

"Now, just a minute . . ."

"Tut, tut . . . don't argue with genius. There'll be nothing to it. Any German will obey a command if it's shouted loudly enough and with enough authority in the voice. It's bred into 'em. From infancy they've been taught *'Befehle sind Befehle,'* and if you look as though you have the authority to give an order they'll click their heels and obey. *Jawohl!* And in no other army in the world does a sergeant major have the power and authority that he has in the German army. A *Feldwebel*, just by looking at him, can make a *Mensch* or any other rating piss in his pants. You watch and see."

Then he held up the uniform for my inspection, and had I not known better, I would have been certain he had somehow obtained a real Luftwaffe uniform. For over a year he had been working on it, and the painstaking care he had lavished on it was apparent. He had rubbed chalk dust into the nap of the blue woolen RAF uniform until it was now an even shade of Luftwaffe gray. Somehow he had got his hands on a bit of yellow cloth, and from this he had made the Luftwaffe piping. From scraps of foil from cigarette packets he had fashioned German eagles for the lapels of the jacket and had also converted the British brass buttons into the silver-hued buttons of a German uniform. The foil had also become *Feldwebel* insignia which, because they were so easily seen, would be the key to this whole venture. With the uniform of any other rank the jackboots would have represented a real problem, but most of the German sergeants fortunately wore ordinary black shoes. But the crowning piece of that whole costume was the Luger holster he had carefully chipped and carved out of a block of wood. The German officers and noncoms wore their Lugers in wooden holsters on their left sides, with the butts facing forward, and John had fashioned a holster that would defy detection except under close scrutiny. The cap had been no problem, for an RAF soft cap was cut on the same lines as its German counterpart, and all that had been necessary was a change in the color and another Nazi eagle. John, dressed in that uniform and standing a few feet away, was a genuine *Feldwebel* in the German Luftwaffe.

"Tomorrow at noon, when the ferrets are out of the camp and when the extra guards are at their midday meal, we, friend Harsh, walk out that gate. I'm taking you and Jerry Finch—he's the bloke who's been watching the gate for me —and the two of these mess mates of ours who draw the long straws. And when we get back to England you four chaps are going to have to stand me drinks whenever I want 'em!"

"Wait a minute," I said. "I've noticed that whenever a German goes out or comes in that gate he's got to have an *Ausweis* . . ."

John cocked an eye at me for a moment. "For a new man you're damned observant," he said, "but I'm way ahead of you on that. Whenever the noted thespian John Agrell plays a role he gets inside the part." He reached into one of the breast pockets of the tunic and extracted a leatherette folder and, flipping it open, flashed before my eyes a short type-written piece of paper with a signature scrawled across the bottom. "Tim Walen made this for me." He grinned.

"Well, I'll be . . . where did he get the typewriter?"

"It's not typewritten." John laughed. "Tim Walen's an artist . . . he did this with a pen and india ink. Here . . . look at it. You'd need a magnifying glass to tell it isn't typed."

That piece of paper was the most amazing example of skillful forgery I had ever seen. It was a short note authorizing *Oberfeldwebel* Otto Schirmer to enter and leave any of the compounds comprising the *Kriegsgefangenenlager Stalag Luft III* and was signed von Lindeiner, *Oberst und Kommandant.*

"From now on just call me Otto." John grinned as I handed the *Ausweis* back to him.

In reality John's scheme was quite sound. There was a constant flow of foot traffic in and out of the wide, barbed-wire gates of the four compounds, guards were always coming and going, and daily groups of volunteer work parties were being escorted through the gates. The Luftwaffe was carefully correct in its observance of the provisions of the Geneva Convention concerning prisoners of war, and so while officers were not forced to work, they were allowed to volunteer for tasks that were, after all, to their own advantage. Once a week a volunteer party of officers would be escorted down to the railway siding to unload the food parcels arriving from the Red Cross via Switzerland, other small parties would be escorted out of the camp to pick up and sort the censored mail for the various compounds, and the sick would be taken out on sick call to the infirmary beyond the gates. Furthermore, no prisoner had heretofore tried John's trick, so there was nothing in the book which the German army used to conduct itself covering this contingency. In the German military mind if no one had issued an order covering a situation, the situation simply did not exist.

A lanky English squadron leader by the name of Somers and a young New Zealander by the name of Cook drew the two long straws in our mess that night, and at noon the next day the four of us, with John striding along beside us, approached the gate. When we were within twenty feet of the gate John bellowed out in pure Prussian, *"Tür auf, Mensch!"*

Dutifully the postern on duty clicked his heels and, as John flashed his *Ausweis* at him, unlocked the gate, and we walked out . . . and no one paid any attention to us.

The previous afternoon I had experienced my first encounter with the "X Organization" that existed inside the wire of Stalag Luft III. This organization, headed by an English squadron leader named Roger Bushell, who had been appointed by the SBO, was in charge of all escape attempts, and any plan for escape had to be submitted to this Big X and his committee. They would consider the plan, pass on its feasibility, and if they approved would back it with all the resources at their disposal. Some months previously John had submitted his plan to them, and they had given it their backing: hence the *Ausweis* with which he had been furnished. On the afternoon before our escape this committee had summoned all five of us to appear before it; we met in a room in one of the barracks around which a security cordon had been thrown, and we were each given a handmade map of the route we were to travel.

"Your best bet is to reach Stettin and there try to get aboard a Swedish freighter." It was Big X speaking. He was a man of medium height, square set, a man who would pass unnoticed in a crowd—until one looked into his face, into his eyes. I, for one, was glad the man was not my enemy. "You're going hard-ass," he continued. "You won't have any forged papers or made-up civilian clothing. You'll have to travel by night and hole up by day. Look at your maps . . . you'll see a rail line in red. Follow this rail line and you'll get to Stettin. Now, about food . . . the only thing we can supply you is four bars of chocolate apiece. You'll have to make it on that."

Up to now I had been taking this whole adventure as some sort of gay lark and had been somewhat amused by all the air of cloak-and-dagger with which it was being surrounded. Then Big X said something which sobered me up and brought the whole thing down to earth.

"I'm sure I don't have to remind you chaps," he said looking at us sharply, "that once you're outside that wire you're no longer under the jurisdiction of the Luftwaffe . . . you are then the responsibility of the Gestapo. And I can tell you from very personal knowledge the Gestapo take a damned bloody dim view of escaping prisoners. Well . . . good luck, chaps!"

And so, with that much preparation we walked out the gate that noon, walked past the *Kommandantur,* past the infirmary, past the guards' barracks. One hundred yards ahead of us the road curved into the woods, and once there, scattered through the pine forest, we would be relatively safe. The first part of our journey would be over. There would not be a roll call until five o'clock that afternoon, so we had five hours in which to put as much mileage as possible between us and the camp. Somehow we smothered the screaming urge to break and run for the woods and continued to walk along at an unconcerned pace. Once more I had the feeling of being naked before mine enemies, and with every step I fully expected to hear a machine gun from one of the guard towers chatter out behind us. We had just reached the bend in the road, and the sheltering trees were within a few paces of us when, coming down the road toward us walked *Hauptmann* Pieber, the *Lageroffizier.* John threw him a smart salute, which he returned in an offhand manner, and then just as he got within a few paces of us he did a double take.

"Oh, no!" he cried incredulously. "Meester Agrell!"

He had not yet learned my name, but as his duties kept him inside the compound most of the time he knew all my companions by sight and name Suddenly snatching out his

Luger and barking "Halt!," he covered us with the weapon. Then with his left arm holding his stomach he doubled up with laughter.

"Ach, Meester Agrell . . . vat a *Feldwebel* you do make! Und Meester Cook und Meester Finch . . . und you, Meester Somers—midout you ve couldn't do. Und for shame —you got dis new man mit his vounds yet strapped up. Ach, vat a shame!"

Suddenly sobering up and waving the pistol menacingly, he barked, "So, turn your leetle army around, Meester Agrell—und back ve go!"

Right then John Agrell proved to me, at least, that he was a born trouper and that someday the stage would hear of him. "All right . . . smartly now, chaps . . . like a guards regiment on parade . . . fall in in columns of fours." Then in the stentorian voice of a drill-ground sergeant major he roared, "Squadron . . . about FACE!"

Smartly the four of us executed the British about-face and, at attention, stood facing down the road back toward the camp.

"Squadron! By the left . . . QUEEK! MARCH!"

And with John barking out the cadence and with our arms swinging in British parade-ground style, we headed back for the camp with Pieber and his Luger following along behind. With our back to him Pieber could not see all of us chewing on our maps. I was glad that I did not also have to chew up a forged *Ausweis*—as it was I didn't think I'd ever get that map down.

By now the whole compound was alerted to what had happened, and as we swung through the gates we were greeted with a loud cheer from six hundred men, a roaring cheer that must have reached Berlin.

John started to march us toward our barracks, but Pieber, still following us, shouted above the hubbub, "Oh, no, Meester Agrell . . . de cooler . . . de cooler!"

As the heavy wooden door of the cell thudded shut behind me and I heard the bolt crash into place I slid down the wall to a sitting position. This was it—ten days on bread and water with nothing but myself for company, and I knew that from this sentence there would be no reprieve. There was no bunk to lie on, no chair to slowly take apart for diversion, there was nothing but four bare walls, a bare floor, and a bare ceiling, and . . . me. And so, on that afternoon, I began rereading every book I had ever read. I tried to recall the plots of these books, every character in them, and every incident that was recorded. It took me four days to get through *War and Peace* alone, and I spent two more days on *The Brothers Karamazov*. I spent a lot of time in dialogues with Socrates, and no matter what theory I would bring up, he would always shoot it full of holes. I had just told him that nobody loves a know-it-all, and that's why he had been forced to drink the hemlock when the door opened and my ten days were up. I'll never know how Socrates wiggled out of my brilliant rejoinder.

16.

Six months later my friend Wally Floody from Toronto entered the room and came over to my bunk, where I lay reading. "Get your ass out of that bunk and come for a walk around the perimeter. God damn it, you're going to be the only able-bodied man in history who ever got bed sores."

I started to demur but soon gave that up. Wally was—and is—a strong-minded, overpowering personality, and I had learned months ago the futility of arguing with him.

"I got something I have to discuss with you—in private," he added with a note of urgency in his voice.

My friendship with this tall, forthright Canadian had grown ever since my second day in the camp. On that day he had also found me lying in my bunk, only that time I had not been reading—I had been commiserating with myself.

"They tell me you're an American," he had stated rather

than asked. The way he made the statement, it sounded like an accusation.

"Yup," I said trying to sound like Gary Cooper as I struggled up to a sitting position.

"Well, I got my monthly letter form from the Germans today," he continued after he had introduced himself, "and tonight I'm writing my wife, Betty, in Toronto. If there's anyone in the States you want to know you're a prisoner, and not dead, I'll get her to contact 'em. In this way they'll know a lot sooner than they will through the Red Cross or the Air Ministry."

The letter form supplied by the Germans was a small sheet of paper only one side of which could be used for a message, and every word had to count if one was to get a message home that would bring some comfort to those one loved. At the time I did not fully appreciate the extent of Wally Floody's generosity, but through this act of his, my sister learned I was alive six weeks before she received the official cable from the Air Ministry. It was a sound basis for a friendship that has lasted through the years.

We had made two circuits of the perimeter inside the barbed wire before Wally broke his thoughtful silence, and then he talked for almost an hour. I did not interrupt him. Had it been anyone else talking, I would have been convinced he had contracted "wire fever" and had gone off his rocker; but I knew Wally to be a serious, sober-minded man, and while what he was outlining was the wildest, most bizarre, and mad plan I had ever heard, I knew Wally himself was not mad.

An escape was to be engineered that would empty this camp of all its six hundred inmates. It was estimated that the preparations for this escape would take a full year, and during this time the entire camp was to be organized on a military basis, every man in the camp would have his duties to carry out, and no one was to be excepted from this effort. Three tunnels going in three different directions were to be dug, and the tunnels were to be of a sophistication never before dreamed of in a prison camp. Wally, because of his years of experience in the mines of northern Ontario, was to design, engineer, and be in overall charge of the actual digging. Minskewitz, the spade-bearded Pole had been captured in 1939 and who had dug tunnels in every camp into which the Germans had thrown him, was to be the architect of the all-important traps to these tunnels. (He had already dug and hidden two of these entrances.) A tailor shop which would convert RAF uniforms into civilian clothing was in the process of being set up by John Agrell. Forged travel permits and false identity cards were to be produced by Tim Walen and the other artists in the camp. And the procuring of all the supplies needed would be left up to a tough, resourceful Australian squadron leader named Willie Williams.

Those in the camp who spoke fluent, idiomatic German were to organize under a Czech, Wally Valenta, and it would be this group's task to immobilize, or "tame," the ferrets who patrolled inside the camp. Pieber, the *Lageroffizier,* would be the responsibility of Bill Webster, an American who had been born in South Africa and reared in England and who had already struck up a useful friendship with *Hauptmann* Pieber.

"Right under our feet," Wally said as we trod along. "Beneath eight inches of topsoil is the whitest, loosest goddam sand you've ever seen. And we're going to bring tons of it up to the surface over the next year. The dispersal of that much telltale sand is going to be up to Hornblower. I'm glad I don't have *his* responsibility."

Hornblower—or more properly, Peter Fanshawe, was a gungho commander in the fleet air arm of the Royal Navy, a career officer who had been shot down early in the war and to whom captivity represented a freezing of his career. The idea of acceptance-of-one's-fate was anathema to Peter Fanshawe. Drake, Frobisher, Hawkins . . . Fanshawe: the

Empire had been founded on such. I was sure Peter would find a means of disposing of that much sand.

Wally talked then of the plan to initiate a concerted and systematic effort to bribe those guards whose greed might outweigh their fear of the Gestapo.

"A levy is to be placed on all the messes in the camp . . . in this way we can hoard a stockpile of chocolate, cigarettes, and powdered coffee with which we hope to barter for those things we can't produce here in the camp. Many of these guards . . . and their wives and children . . . haven't seen chocolate or real coffee in years. And the German cigarette ration is down to three a day."

He then talked for some moments of the tunnels that were to be dug. ". . . we've decided to dig three of them. I wanted to call them The Father, The Son, and The Holy Ghost, but Roger Bushell vetoed that. He pointed out we're going to need all the help we can get—from whatever source —and that we'd better not start out by making the Almighty cross with us. They're to be called Tom, Dick, and Harry. The shafts are to go straight down thirty feet. We've got to go that deep to out-range the sound detectors the goons have ringed the camp with. Of course it will be obvious to the Germans that if we are tunneling we would do so from the barracks closest to the wire. But we can't help it . . . as it is, the laterals of these tunnels will be over four hundred feet in order to reach into the woods."

"But why three tunnels?" I finally interrupted. "Why not concentrate on just one?"

"Because if we're going to empty this camp of six hundred men in one night we're going to need that many escape holes. Also it's inconceivable that the Germans won't find at least one. We may think they're stupid . . . but we can't base our thinking on that premise. They may even find two —but the third one gives us a slight break in the odds. And God knows we're going to need all the breaks we can get."

"Who dreamed up this wild idea?"

"Oh, I suppose Roger Bushell started it," Wally said. "He hates the Germans with a hatred that's almost pathological. He's escaped three times, you know, and the last time the Gestapo caught him they kept him in one of their jails for three months. He won't say much about it, but they must have given him hell. He's got a theory that at the end of his war we should salt over Germany—as the Romans did Carthage—and create an uninhabitable desert here in the heart of Europe. He knows, of course, that probably every one of the six hundred of us will be recaptured . . . but he's determined to create as big a flap as possible right here in Germany."

"It'll cause a flap all right," I said, shaking my head. "And I should think that Roger, of all people, would realize that the Gestapo have a particularly nasty way of flapping."

"Oh, screw the Gestapo. They're just Germans too."

"Maybe so. But just how the hell do you guys plan to secure any such effort as this?"

"I dunno," he replied. And then a grin spread over his rugged features. "That's going to be your problem. You, my friend, are going to be in charge of security."

I didn't exactly blow my stack, but I did lose my cool, and for fifteen solid minutes I unburdened myself of my opinion of Wally Floody, Roger Bushell, Wing Commander Harry Day, and anyone else connected with this madness. "For over a year I've been getting more and more fed up with the military mind . . . and this is military thinking at its worst and bloodiest. You crazy bastards are going to get the whole lot of us shot! You know what this is? It's as stupid as a lion tamer sticking his head in a lion's mouth and then kicking the lion in the balls!"

By now I was almost shouting at Wally. But I might as well have saved my breath. He hadn't heard a word I had said.

"This is a military operation," he stated, not even bothering to answer my tirade, "and Wings Day in his capacity as senior British officer in this camp has ordered you to secure the operation. You are to pick out two hundred men to help you. Good luck."

"But why me?" I asked, still fuming. "There are wing commanders and squadron leaders in this camp who are more capable of trying to do this impossible job than I am."

"Oh, yeah? And how many of them have spent twelve years in prison?" Suddenly he grinned at me again. "We need a man on this job with some experience."

During the course of our friendship I had confided in Wally that part of my past . . . and now that confidence was coming home to roost.

"I told Wings and Roger that if I was going to spend the next year or so of my life prowling around down in the bowels of Germany I wanted a man topside, protecting me, in whom I could feel some trust. Naturally I didn't reveal to them what you told me in confidence. I just told them I wanted you on this security job."

"Thanks," I sneered. "Thanks a hell of a lot."

"You know something?" Wally chuckled, "you're probably the only man in the world who got a job because he's an ex-convict."

"Very funny. I'm dying with laughter."

"Well, anyway, you and I have an appointment in the morning, right after *Appell,* with Wings and Roger. Group Captain Massey will be there too. He just got back from the hospital again."

17.

The next morning after *Appell* when Wally
and I entered Wing Commander Day's room
we found him seated behind a table, facing the door. On his
right sat the actual senior British officer in the camp, Group
Captain Massey, who because of his wound had delegated his
authority to Wings Day, and on his left sat Squadron Leader
Roger Bushell. At first the whole arrangement—three senior
officers seated as a tribunal—seemed somewhat staged and
unnecessarily dramatic, especially in contrast to the infor-
mality of a prison camp; but I was not in the room long before I realized these three had just happened to be sitting
that way and were not trying to impress anyone. They didn't
have to.

Group Captain H. M. Massey was an older man, having
been a pilot in the first World War and a member of the old
Royal Flying Corps. He had been a station commander in
Bomber Command in this war and as such was not supposed

to fly on missions, but his curiosity had got the better of him, and he had gone along on a bombing mission just for a look-see. However, his luck ran out, the plane he was in was coned, and he came clumping down on German soil in a parachute. On the way down he picked up a particularly nasty flak wound in his right foot, a wound that defied healing and one which was giving him considerable trouble. The Germans, being a military people, are extremely rank-conscious, and Massey, being the equivalent of a colonel—or *Oberst*—received a lot of solicitude from his captors. On frequent occasions they would send him off to one of their military hospitals, where specialists could have a look at his wound. It was following one of these trips that the Germans offered to repatriate him in order that his foot could receive the attention it required. Massey had not exactly sneered at this offer but with great dignity had informed the Germans that he was quite content to wait until the triumphant British armies entered Germany and he could return home in style befitting one of his rank. On the surface the Germans wrote this off as a bit of British bravado, but underneath it did give them pause. The effect on the morale of hundreds of junior officers under him was terrific, and understandably Massey had the deep respect of each of his subordinates.

Wing Commander Harry Day, both in physical appearance and temperament, was in marked contrast to his superior. He was an exceedingly tall man, almost gaunt, and he had the lean and hungry look of "yon Cassius." He had been commanding officer of a squadron of Blenheim reconnaissance bombers and had been shot down during the first months of the war. As a career officer he too was tasting the bitter gall of being frozen in his present rank due to ill luck. But beneath his grim and forbidding exterior Day was an ebullient and gregarious person, a devil-may-care man who believed implicitly in the curative powers of Scotch whisky for any malady or woeful situation; it was he who pointed out that for all RAF veterans the war would be a lasting boon: "The fighter defense of Malta will give any of us an excuse to celebrate—at any time—for the rest of our lives."

Harry Day held an implacable hatred of the Germans and all things Germanic, and one of his finest moments— one which showed what was at the core of the man—came about one morning when for some forgotten reason the Gestapo were again threatening to shoot every tenth one of us. Drawing himself up to his full height, he impaled the Gestapo with an icy stare and demanded, "Has it ever occurred to you bloody people that we are going to win this war?"

It can't be said that this exactly made the Gestapo quake in their boots, but at least they did not carry out their threat —that day.

Of the three it was undoubtedly Roger Bushell who carried within himself the greatest hatred of the enemy. I never found out what the Gestapo had done to him during the time they held him prisoner, but whatever it was, they had turned him into a vengeful, bitter man who was out to do in all Germans by any means possible. Actually, underneath his forbidding exterior Roger was a charming, cultivated gentleman, but nature had bestowed on him a visage that can only be described as sinister. Years before he had been involved in a skiing accident in Switzerland that had left a wicked-looking scar on his face and one eye with a perpetual droop. He was a brilliant man and one with a shrewd grasp of psychology. The Germans would soon learn it had been a black day for them when they had captured him.

It was these three men I faced when I walked into Harry Day's room with Wally Floody that morning. Wings wasted no time in getting down to the business at hand and quickly outlined the project that Wally had already filled me in on.

"So long as I breathe," Wings stated, "no officer—nor group of officers—under my command will ever let up in the war against the enemy . . . especially this enemy. And just because we're prisoners doesn't mean we're going to relax and sit out this war in idleness. We intend to give these Huns a bad time! And you, Harsh, are charged with the job of securing this effort. If any bastard—or group of bastards—gets in your way or hampers your work, I want to know about it. I'll have 'em court-martialed to the last man once this war is over! This is a military operation, and I expect it to be carried out as such."

Group Captain Massey then spoke briefly for a moment, touching on the duties of a captured officer as laid down in King's Regulations for Air. "I'm afraid you may run into a few officers in this camp who think just because they're prisoners they've done their duty and are going to retire. You may have to persuade 'em back to a sense of duty. The methods you use are up to you—we'll back you."

It was then Roger Bushell's turn to talk, and fixing me with his scarred eye, he began slowly, "There isn't a bloody one of us in this camp who isn't living on borrowed time," he said quietly. "By rights every one of us should be dead. And the only reason the good Lord preserved us is so we can give these blasted Huns as much hell as we can. None of us in this room is stupid—how many people do we really think we're going to get back to England? Damned few . . . we all know that. But, by God, we're going to give these Germans a bad time! Can you picture their faces when they march in here some day for the morning roll call . . . and there isn't a damned soul in the camp? God, I'd almost stay behind just to see that sight! We're going to give these Huns as much trouble as would a division of assault troops landing on the beaches of France . . . and we're going to do it working right here in their own stinking bosoms. These Germans are going to learn—from us—just what sort of foe they're up against. And the whole damn lot of us may die in the attempt . . . but, by God, we'll die as men . . . and officers doing our duty. I'm not trying to be dramatic, but all of us in this room know the type of pool the Gestapo plays—we're just going to play a little dirtier pool, that's all. I tell you, Harsh, we in this camp are going to cause such a God-awful flap in this bloody country that they'll never forget it!"

Later, after Wally and I had left the room and were out walking the circuit where we could talk in safety, I started chuckling to myself.

"What's so funny?" he growled.

"Me," I said. "D'you remember that wonderful passage in *The Wizard of Oz* . . . when Dorothy and her crew are approaching the castle of the Wicked Witch of the West? They have to get into that castle, but the gate and the draw-bridge across the moat are guarded by the Wicked Witch's ferocious soldiers. Dorothy and the rest of them are hidden in the woods, casing the joint, and worrying how they're going to get past those soldiers. And then the Cowardly Lion starts growling deep in his throat, and then he gets up and beats himself on his chest with his paw.

" 'I'll get us in there!' he growls. 'I'll go down there and tear 'em limb from limb . . . I'll chew 'em up! I'll . . .'

" 'Oh, Cowardly Lion!' Dorothy cries. 'What can we do to help?'

"And suddenly the Cowardly Lion comes back to earth with a thump, and remembers who he is. 'Talk me out of it,' he says lamely. Well, Wally Floody, you've just seen *The Wizard of Oz* reversed. You've just seen the Cowardly Lion get talked into going down and trying to cope with the Wicked Witch's ferocious soldiers. Y'know . . . when I went in that room I was all prepared to tell those three hunks of brass that I wanted no part of their silly, suicidal 'military operation.' But after a few minutes with them . . . well, I guess I'd have looked pretty ridiculous telling them that. But, you, you bastard . . . you got me into this. You're going to have to stand me drinks when we get back to London."

An American air force colonel, Bob Clark, had already devised and had in operation a security system for the camp that worked well. He would have been the obvious man to have taken over the added task of securing the tunnels, but the rumor had come to us that soon the Americans were to be separated from us British prisoners and placed in a new camp of their own; so it was decided that one of the RAF people who would remain in the camp should be given this task.

For the rest of that day Bob Clark and I prowled the camp together; we made numerous circuits just inside the warning wire to note the disposition of the guards in the watchtowers with their machine guns and binoculars; we walked past the main gate, and I made mental notes of the manner in which the ferrets entered and left the compound; we prowled between the barracks, searching out the few blind spots from the towers. For the first time I was seeing the whole setup with new eyes, and the more I saw, the more discouraged I became. Bob had done an excellent job of securing the camp with his crew of American "stooges" but I soon realized how much tighter the security was going to have to be from now on. It seemed almost hopeless that a tunneling operation such as these people had in mind could be carried out undetected, but I knew only too well that nothing I could say would dissuade them from this attempt . . . and that, like it or not, I was going to have to protect it.

The next morning a meeting was called in Roger's room of all the people who had been appointed to key positions in the project. As I approached the barracks I noticed the handful of security stooges Bob Clark had obviously put on duty to cover this meeting; obvious was the key word, for the men loitering around on the outside of the building could be nothing other than lookouts. I made a mental note that from now on that would have to be corrected.

Roger was speaking as I entered the room after knocking. "Sit down," he barked. "You're late." This was to be a British military-style operation, and Roger left no doubt as to that. "I've decided on three tunnels," he continued after I had found a seat, "because I like the asymmetry of the figure three. The Germans will probably find one of these tunnels—maybe even two—but the third gives us a slight break. When they find one of these elaborate tunnels they'll think we've put everything we've got into it. And if they find the second, they'll know damn' well we have. And that's just what I want 'em to think. And that brings up something else . . . from here on out everyone of us—God help us—has got to think as the Germans think. We've got to get inside their minds and stay one jump ahead of 'em.

"From this moment on I never want to hear the word *tunnel* mentioned in this camp . . . I don't care if the speaker is dead certain no ferret can overhear him . . . the word is to be expunged from our vocabularies. These three *things* have code names—Tom and Dick and Harry."

Rising to his feet and folding his arms across his chest, Roger then faced this roomful of men from all over the British Empire and most of the occupied countries of Europe. Tom goes out of 123 block under the west wire, Dick goes out of 122 block and also under the west wire, and then Harry . . . well, somehow I have the hunch that Harry is going to be our boy . . . Harry goes out of 104 block, heads under the *Vorlager,* under the cooler, under the road, and comes up in the woods in front of the camp—a total distance of four hundred feet . . ."

A groan came from those in the room who were hearing this for the first time.

"Groan, you bastards"—Roger grinned—"but I'm thinking like a German now . . . and 104 block is the last one the Hun would suspect us to dig a tunnel from."

"You just said a dirty word, Roger," Willie Williams reminded him.

"You're right . . . and let that be the last time that word is used around here."

Roger then turned the meeting over to Wally Floody,

and for some moments Wally elaborated on the details of the tunnels: from the thirty-foot shafts the laterals were to go straight out, and they would be no larger than absolutely necessary, affording no more than mere crawl space for the largest man in the camp. As the laterals extended it would be necessary to pump air into them in order for the diggers to breathe, and he announced that Jens Mueller, the Norwegian, was working on a pump system using bellows made from canvas kit bags. Electric lights were to be strung the length of the shafts. (At last some use would be found for the drum of electric wiring that Red Noble, the rambunctious Canadian, had stolen from the German workmen who had still been at work within the camp when it had been opened.) And then Wally spoke of the loose, white sand through which the tunnels were to be dug and which would be something all of us would have to live with.

"Every foot of the laterals is going to have to be shored against cave-ins," he announced, "and getting rid of that much sand up here in the compound is going to be a screaming pain in the ass to all of us."

The meeting was then turned over to Minskewitz, and in his heavy Polish accents he described to us the traps of the three tunnels: the entrance to Tom was to be through a water catch basin in the shower room of 123 block. At least six inches always stood in this sump, a fact which would throw the Germans off the scent, but he had found that by bailing out this water and fashioning a false sliding side panel to the sump, access could be gained to the ground beneath the barracks. Then, when closed up, the cracks around the panel could be sealed with a mixture of soap and sand, water could be again allowed to stand in the sump, and the Germans would probably never find it.

A note of apology seemed to creep into his voice as he described the trap to Dick in 122 block; it was as though an artist was describing a piece of his work of which he was not especially proud. This trap was just a fitted square of concrete which would plug up the hole that had been dug through the cement floor. But the trap was in a dark corner behind a chimney, and sweeping dust over the cracks when the tunnel was closed could prevent its detection.

However, in describing the trap to Harry, the artist's pride returned to his voice: this tunnel entrance was to be under a stove in one of the rooms of 104 block. The pot-bellied stove sat on a tile base, and he had removed the tiles, cut through the cement under them to the ground beneath, and reset the tiles on a trap door. With the fired-up stove in place that would be the least likely spot for the Germans to suspect a tunnel entrance.

When Minskiewitz finished telling of the traps, the floor was turned over to Hornblower to tell of the system he had devised for the dispersal of the many tons of sand. Typical of Hornblower, he didn't tell us, he showed us. From cloth he had designed two long bags, looking like huge sausage casings, which would fit down inside a man's trousers and hang in place from a cord around the wearer's neck. The bottom of these sausage casings was fitted with a pin which could be released by pulling on a string which would come up into the pockets of the trousers; thus, walking along, the wearer could distribute his load of sand over a wide area, and a man shuffling along behind could scuff the sand into the topsoil. It was an indecently brilliant idea, and as each sausage skin would hold a half bucket of sand, it was beginning to look like we might actually dispose of all that white stuff.

Roger then resumed the floor, and after summing up all that had been said he—in front of all these officers who would be the key personnel in this project—dumped the security for it squarely in my lap. "No one moves in this camp," he continued, "no trap is to be opened, not a grain of sand is to be dispersed, no hidey-holes are to be opened, no workshops are to be activated . . . nothing . . . until George gives the signal. I hope this is understood. It had bloody well better be . . . for there's a court-martial yawning wide open back in England once this was is over for anyone who disobeys an order."

He then announced that work would commence one week from this day and that I would therefore have one week during which to perfect a security system. On this note he dismissed the meeting.

I had already selected George McGill, an athletic Canadian, and McGarr, a rugged South African, to help me manage the two-hundred-man security force that would be under us. I knew that they felt as deeply as I did the awesome responsibility that had been shoved onto us. To many of the officers in the camp this wasn't just a lark or one more means of annoying the Germans; to many of the men who had been here since 1939 this escape was a matter of life or death. This was especially true of the Polish officers, for many of them had been active in politics in their country before the war, they were under no false dreams as to what would happen to them should they be taken by the Russians. The discovery by the Germans of the mass grave of hundreds of Polish officers who had been murdered by the Russians at Katyn left no doubt that their only chance for survival lay in escape and making their way to western Europe.

All of these thoughts crowded in on me and weighed me down as I prowled the camp that day with McGill and McGarr. Often in my life I have felt inadequate for the tasks fate has put before me, but I don't think ever before had I felt that sense of inadequacy quite as keenly.

For the next week McGill, McGarr, and I hardly slept a wink, we were together almost every hour out of each twenty-four, we were together even when one of us had to go to the *Abort,* and we practically lived in one another's hip pockets. But at the end of the week we had perfected a security system that held up under the probing of the Luftwaffe, the searching of the German Internal *Abwehrkraft,* and the more thorough—and ruthless—probing of the Gestapo. First of all, a round-the-clock, unobtrusive watch of the gate was established in order that the duty officer at the hub of the system would know instantaneously who entered or left the camp. Then the camp was divided into square, numbered sections, and the whereabouts of any German would be known during every minute he was inside the camp. A signal system was devised—the way a certain garment was hanging on a clothes line, the manner in which an empty Red Cross carton was placed on an incinerator, the way in which a certain door had been left ajar—and through these means we had immediate communication all over the camp. McGill, being a big-league baseball fan, and I leaned heavily on the signal systems used by all big-league teams, and McGarr, being a South African, soon learned more about baseball than he thought he ever would. By patching up, by improvising as we went along, and through quick thinking on the part of all two hundred Allied officers engaged in the security system, we made it work. From the first week on, through all the ensuing months during which we worked and lived so closely together, I got to know and respect both McGill and McGarr. Through the trying conditions and the nerve-racking moments, I got to know their minds, and their hearts . . . their dreams and their aspirations, and I came to see what an influence for good and for sanity two such men could be in the coming world.

Later, when the Gestapo murdered them, something within me also died. I am not trying to be dramatic. This is a simple statement of fact. If right-wing, fascist brutes such as the Gestapo—filled as they were with the blind belief that their cause was just, inflamed by intemperate rhetoric, and convinced through warped logic that what they were doing was a patriotic duty—could murder two such promising, decent young men as McGarr and McGill, what hope was there for the human race? And at the time I was convinced that all this would happen again at some future date; for if my reading of history has taught me anything it is that man never has learned from his past.

The murder of these and many other friends who had been engaged in this project was part of the aftermath that Roger had forseen. And the fact that I, by mistake, was saved along with a handful of other key personnel, is one of the great ironies of my life.

18.

For over a year the work progressed on the tunnels, and whenever possible we worked around the clock. Looking back on that period of my life, I seemed to have spent most of the time with my heart in my mouth. During the year we lost Dick, the tunnel whose trap Minskewitz had been least satisfied with. I was proud at the time that it was not through negligence on the part of any of the security force that the Germans found the tunnel, but rather through the blind luck of one of the ferrets stumbling onto the entrance. At first a great gloom settled over the camp at the loss of this tunnel, the shaft of which had already reached the wire. But as Roger had hoped and predicted, the loss redounded to our benefit. Finding that elaborate tunnel with all its supplies convinced the Germans we had expended all our energies and contraband resources on it, and for two months they slackened their vigilance. During these months we dug with renewed vigor and concentrated all our efforts on one tunnel—Harry, the trap of which was under the red-hot stove.

Then came the day when it was estimated the shaft of the tunnel was safely into the woods, and cautiously, a few inches at a time, the upward shaft toward freedom was started. After the first few feet of the upward shaft had been dug, a two-foot steel rod was pushed straight up, and the digging continued as long as this rod met resistance. This gingerly probing was continued every few inches after that. And then came the moment when the jubilant word was passed back that the rod had broken clear and that the tunneler had spied daylight through the tiny hole. The tunnel Harry was completed!

Three officers holding degrees in mathematics had been assigned the task of keeping the tunnel straight and at a uniform depth and also of estimating how far it would have to be dug to reach the safety of the woods. They had made this latter calculation by means of crude triangulation. Now at least freedom from the barbed wire of the camp was within our grasp.

There was only one disappointment: six hundred men could not be got out of one tunnel in one night, but it was estimated that two hundred and twenty could.

"We can't win all the time," Roger said dourly, but, then brightening, added, "At least, two hundred men scattered across the countryside should shake the Huns to their bloody tits!"

It was now the fourteenth of March, and it was decided to wait until the night of the twenty-fourth before opening the tunnel.

"There'll be no moon that night," Roger reasoned, "and as the spring thaw has started, maybe this layer of snow will be melted by then."

Friday, March 24, 1944, dawned bright and clear, and despite a strong March wind, the weather had moderated and the snow had melted. It was hoped the wind would continue into the night, for it would help dissipate any noise that might be made during the escape. The excitement in the camp was electric, and the security people had a full job keeping it muffled all during the day. The selection of the two hundred and twenty men had been made, and they were to move into 104 block before lockup time, bringing with them their mocked-up civilian clothing, their forged travel permits, and their identity cards. This many men converging on 104 block just at dusk had to be regulated and policed carefully, for if the Germans were aroused and sprung a quick search at this time all our year-long effort would end in a ghastly nightmare.

But all went smoothly, and just as the moonless night engulfed the camp the order went down to the three tunnelers on duty to break through the two feet of top soil and open the tunnel. No one seemed to breathe as we waited.

And then the word came back—the tunnel was fifteen feet short of the woods!

"Oh, God . . . no!" seemed to be the one cry of despair that escaped from six hundred men.

Immediately the plans had to be altered, for there could be no turning back now; there were no feasible means of closing the hole and resuming digging, so it was now or never. But this would mean the escapees would have to be slipped out at intervals when the patrolling sentry had his back turned, and it would also mean that the number of men who could be got out during the hours of darkness would be sharply reduced. It was quickly decided that the Poles and the other Europeans who knew the customs would go first and then, as time permitted, would go those who had spent the most time in the preparations for this night. Wing Commander Day decreed that Roger, because he had been the guiding force behind this project, was to go first. Many of the key personnel would have to go last, as time permitted, for their services and experience would be needed in this emergency.

Roger and twenty others had been slipped out at spaced intervals when another bit of sour luck struck. On this of all nights the RAF chose to stage an air raid on Breslau, only forty miles to the south, and as the warning sirens sounded the Germans pulled the master switch, plunging the entire camp into complete blackout. Instead of benefitting the escape the blackout delayed it further, for during these blackouts the guard patrolling on the outside of the wire was doubled, and we had to wait until all this flurry of guard activity settled into its routine. Also, while we had anticipated a claustrophobia, the utter, stygian darkness of the tunnel multiplied this sensation dangerously. The cases of blind, unreasoning panic had to be dealt with swiftly and ruthlessly.

One man in his crazed fear tried to crawl back over the stretched-out bodies of the men behind him, and there was real danger that in his panic he would knock loose the shoring and collapse a whole section of the tunnel. A length of rope was passed down, he was grabbed by those nearest him, and finally, trussed and bound, he was passed back up to the surface. As soon as he was brought up into the room his panic melted, and he slunk shamefacedly off into the barracks. He was a squadron leader who had been awarded the DFC and bar, but claustrophobia is no respecter of ribbons for bravery.

Another man, halfway through the tunnel, suddenly froze into a near-catatonic state, his body rigid and his wide-open eyes glazed over in unseeing fear. He represented no real problem—other than the delay he was causing—for his rigid body was quickly passed back and brought up to the entrance.

However, the unexpected claustrophobia that suddenly appeared in a large, powerful Australian was another matter. The man had been a champion swimmer in his native land, and in the cramped confines of the tunnel enough men could not be got around him to truss him into harmlessness.

He was finally knocked cold with the handle of a digging tool, and his inert, unconscious body was quickly passed back to the tunnel mouth.

In spite of all the obstacles, eighty men had been got out when one of the escapees made a noise and alerted a sentry. The alarm went up, the flap was on, and this part of the escape was over.

During the roll call Floody, Fanshawe, and I, along with twenty-two others, were told to step out of rank and line up to one side. We were the ones the ferrets suspected of complicity in the escape, and as the Gestapo called out my name . . . well, I still don't like to remember that moment. But instead of shooting us out of hand, they herded us into a punishment camp at Belaria, twenty-five miles away.

It was there that we first began to receive rumors as to what had happened to the eighty men we had got out that dark, windy night, and it was three months before we learned the true story. Twenty-seven men had been captured by the civil police and the *Abwehrkraft* and had been returned to the camp. Three of the escapees had actually made it back to England and, as could have been predicted, they were all Europeans. A Dutchman was able to contact the various underground organizations, which finally got him to England via Spain. The other two, both Norwegians, had got to Stettin, boarded a Swedish freighter, and were back in England within a few days. The remaining fifty had been captured by the Gestapo, held in various Gestapo jails for a day or two, and then simply taken out, shot in the back of the head, and buried in unmarked graves.

19.

The episodes, the triumphs, and the tragedies that took place during this year of my life have come to be known as "The Great Escape," from the book of that title by Paul Brickhill. Paul had also been in the camp and had of course participated in the events; he had been a newspaper man before the war, and his trained eye and memory helped him to see and remember all the episodes and the names of the people involved in them. His is the definitive, documented, and historically accurate chronicle of this bit of World War II. It was from this book that John Sturges, the Hollywood director, made the amazingly accurate motion picture of the same name.

In these pages I have not tried to rewrite Paul's book, but because this is a personal chronicle, I have attempted to set forth simply how these happenings affected me and my future and how they helped mold my attitudes and thinking.

By the very nature of what he is trying to do, an autobiographer is in an ambivalent position: he must write of the past within the framework of that period, and he must do this despite the fact that his entire attitude and position may have changed diametrically during the ensuing years. At the time of The Great Escape I had grave doubts as to the wisdom or worth of trying to engineer a mass prison escape from the heart of Germany. At this date, after the passage of all these years and because of the events that have transpired during these years, I consider The Great Escape to have been an act of typical military madness, a futile, empty gesture and a needless sacrifice of fifty lives.

I realize these matters are all in the point of view. I have many friends who were also in Stalag Luft III and who today are convinced that what we did was a brave, necessary, and heroic thing. I can agree with them that Nazi Germany had to be destroyed and that Hitler had to be stopped. And I further believe that World War II was the last war fought that could not have been prevented by reason and sanity. But I do not believe that what we did affected the eventual outcome of that war by so much as one tittle.

*   *   *

The Germans kept us in the maximum security camp at Belaria until the late winter of 1945. For some months the Russians had been coiled on the east banks of the Vistula River while they regrouped their forces, brought up supplies, and prepared themselves for the final onslaught into the heartland of Germany. Then, after first signaling the Polish underground to start the uprising in the Warsaw ghetto, they stormed across the Vistula in massive waves of men and armor, and Armageddon was reaching for its climax.

For some weeks, as the Russian advance approached Silesia, rumors had been thick in the camp that our captors planned to march us westward. All Allied air force officers were to be corralled in one place, there guarded by the SS, and Hitler was to use us as bargaining pawns while he negotiated with the victors who were now crowding in from both fronts. So the rumors went.

Most of us scoffed at these rumors: "They aren't able to do it . . . not with the quality of troops they're now having to use as guards."

"Ridiculous . . ."

"They'll be too busy fleeing the Russians to bother with us."

"Even if they try it, if we drag our feet the Russians will overtake us within a few miles . . ."

It would seem, after all the years most of us had spent in Germany, that we would have realized that on occasion the Germans could rise to the "impossible." They marched us out of the camp.

We had made the fatal military mistake of underestimating an enemy, and none of us had prepared himself for this ordeal. Looking back on it, however, it's hard to see what we could have done. There wasn't a sound pair of marching boots left among us, our clothing was in tatters, and for some months we had been living on starvation rations. Someday, somehow, someone will write the definitive treatise on starvation. In these United States, which has the largest garbage cans in the world, the word starvation is synonymous with *hunger,* or *good appetite.* There's a world of difference.

We were starving, and we all had lost weight to a dangerous degree and this despite the pounds of lice each one of us was carrying. It had been too cold to wash or shave. No wonder the lice had found us.

At dawn on the morning of January 28, 1945, with a blizzard howling across eastern Silesia, the Germans started marching us westward. A gung ho Luftwaffe major was in charge of the one hundred and fifty prisoners and the thirty guards who were marched out of the camp that bitter cold morning.

We were lined up in the *Vorlager*, a roll call was taken, and then the major shouted at us above the whistling of the wind: "We do this in order to protect you from the Russians!"

For the rest of the march he was known among us as Humpty Dumpty, for it was Humpty Dumpty who had said to Alice, "A word means exactly what I intend for it to mean . . . neither more nor less."

With this pronouncement, the major gave up his attempts at English and reverted to German—which we understood better than his English, anyway. There was to be no escaping, no falling out by the wayside, and no feigning of sickness, and he was under orders to shoot any of us who disobeyed these rules. In other words, he was going to "protect" us from the Russians if he had to shoot every one of us to do it.

Just before the major bellowed, *"Rechts raum! Marsch!"* the Germans opened the door to a small warehouse, and we were allowed to help ourselves to all the Red Cross food parcels we could carry. Undoubtedly the Germans had intended this food for their own use, but the rapidity of the Russian advance had upset any plans they may have had for it, so rather than let it fall to the Russians, we were allowed to have what was rightfully ours. The sight of all this food which had been hoarded here during the months of our starvation filled most of us with a new bitterness toward our captors; but there wasn't time to luxuriate in this emotion— we were all too busy trying to load ourselves down with everything we could carry.

Through the years a friendship had grown between Wally Floody, Kingsley Brown, and me. I knew what was at the core of these two rugged Canadians, and I liked what

I found there. The three of us quickly decided that our best bet for survival lay in pooling our forces and sticking together through whatever might lay ahead.

"Chocolate," Wally said, stuffing his pockets with the specially prepared, hard D-bars. "We can carry more of this than anything."

"And cigarettes," Brownie added, also stuffing his pockets. "We can trade 'em for food."

Most of our fellow prisoners were loading themselves down with entire Red Cross food parcels. I still wonder how far they thought they were going to trudge through the blizzard carrying such weighty burdens. As Wally, Brownie, and I marched out the gate our pockets were bulging, but our hands were free—except for the tins of bully beef we were wolfing.

The major had promised us that once a day during the march an army field kitchen was to meet us and that we would be given an ample quantity of hot soup and a half loaf of bread per man. The methodical Germans had undoubtedly planned and cut orders for this arrangement, but the chaos of German defeat was beginning to make meaningless most plans and orders. Chaos and panic and pandemonium are self-feeding, like a brush fire, and as the Russian advance pressed closer this chaos would spread. We had some hope in those promised field kitchens, but little faith.

Our hope would have been stronger had our guards also been dependent on the field kitchens, but just outside Belaria they had commandeered a farm wagon drawn by two sturdy horses, and all their packs, blankets, and field rations were piled onto this wagon. The fact that these field kitchens actually appeared on five separate occasions during the hell of that march is minor miracle.

On first arriving in Belaria almost a year earlier we had all acquired Klim powdered milk tins from the Red Cross packages and we wore them attached by a loop of string to our belts. These, with a tin spoon issued by the Germans, were our sole culinary utensils. But these two items sufficed, for with them we were amply prepared to take on anything liquid, hot, and edible that might appear.

By midafternoon of the first day those who had over-burdened themselves with tins of food had jettisoned every item except those they could carry crammed into their pockets. Just to keep plodding onward through that accumulating snow required all the strength one could muster.

The first night the Germans crowded all one hundred and fifty of us into a barn and after shouting, "*Nicht rauchen!*" barred the door. The "no smoking" order from them was superfluous, for it was a rule we imposed on ourselves; we were under no illusions as to the Germans unbarring the door should all that hay catch fire. A night in a hay barn with a blizzard howling outside may conjure up in some minds a picture of snug comfort, but one hundred and fifty men crowded into that small barn gave it more the reality of the Black Hole of Calcutta.

In my mind today that march is a pastiche of cold, hunger, human misery, and frostbite. On the second day the blizzard stopped, and then the wind shifted south, and the snow began to melt. It seemed that even the gods were against us, for the slush through which we had to plod was even worse than the snow. What socks we had were now fishnets, just a collection of holes fastened together, and our worn boots had started to rot and burst their stitching, and the soles flapped with every step.

Within a few days our guards were almost as bad off as we were. For the most part they were older men, late conscripts who were considered too aged for active front line duty but good enough to guard us. One afternoon Brownie, who spoke idiomatic German, fell into conversation with one of these old boys who had been plodding along beside us for the past hour. He was a school teacher from Bavaria who had fought in the Kaiser's army in World War I, so war and defeat and all the misery of defeat were no strangers to him.

"Hitler," he stated with conviction at one point in the conversation, "is a madman. This I knew . . . and many other Germans knew it too. But what could we do? He appealed to people's emotions . . . to their baser instincts . . . their pride and their fears and their nationalism. And when people start thinking with their emotions, and not their reason . . . ach, it's no good!"

The strap on the heavy World War I Mauser rifle they had given him was beginning to gall his thin shoulders, and Brownie helped him. For almost two hours Brownie trudged along with the old man's rifle slung over his own shoulder. Then the major spied him; the scream of Teutonic rage he let out would have warmed the heart of Bismarck could he have heard it.

"Someday I shoot that major maybe . . . no?" the old man whispered as he took his rifle back from Brownie.

"Yes," Brownie agreed, "a *vortreffliche* idea."

The main east-west highways and the *autobahns* were reserved for strictly military traffic, so we were marched along dirt secondary roads and within a few days were caught up and engulfed in the backwash of this German debacle. This was truly *Götterdämmerung*. The roads were swarming with slave laborers from all the occupied countries of Europe trying to reach their homes in the west, with German civilian refugees from East Prussia and Lower Silesia, with women and children and dogs and cats and nuns and priests . . . and they had their moveable possessions in carts, wheelbarrows, and wheelchairs. In some of the wheelchairs were old people, too aged or infirm to walk. This was the face of war, the real war with the false mask removed. Gone now were the blaring bands and the banners, the massed Nazi rallies in the *Sportspalast*, the thundering roars of *Heil Hitler!* and the swelling, unified cheer, *Sieg Heil!* The mass hysteria was now massed tears.

These were just people now, all members of the human race, and no one cared very much about the national origin of someone with whom he was sharing a crust of bread— we were just trying to stay alive, and there wasn't time to worry about such inconsequential matters. We shared among us the common levelers of cold, hunger, lice, misery, and despair.

For several days the major drove himself hoarse trying to keep his charges separate from the swarm of refugees, but he soon realized his problem was bigger than he was, and finally he too just trudged along with the rest of us. Occasionally though, his sense of duty and his Naziness would flame up from the embers, and he would reassert himself in bellowed orders to the guards to keep us bunched up. By now no one paid much attention.

Despite my own misery this tall, undoubtedly capable German military man fascinated me, or rather the metamorphosis that was slowly taking place within him did. By the looks of him, and from his actions, he had probably been an early member of the Nazi Party, a staunch believer in the infallibility of *Der Führer* and a rabid exponent of the superiority of the "pure Aryan." But slowly, from day to day, there was beginning to creep into his awareness the inescapable certainty that Nazi Germany was beaten. A cold analysis of the facts would have made him realize this a long time ago, but he had closed his mind to these facts. It took the sight of all these refugees to bring this awareness crashing into his mind. It took the sight of an old Jewess from Poland sharing her crust of bread with a once-proud *Junker* from East Prussia . . . and maybe it took the sight of one of his prisoners sharing the burden of a rifle with one of his guards.

But he was a strong-minded man and he was a long way from admitting that the Nazi tenets in which he zealously believed could be wrong. No, this was an unmistakable example of Evil triumphing over Good—something he thought could never happen; but there was no escaping now the fact that it was indeed happening.

One midmorning, after a particularly ghastly night in an overcrowded barn at a little town called Gross Zelten, one of our members fell by the wayside. I knew him, of course: he had been a Spitfire pilot, and while he was only twenty years old, he was already a veteran and one of the heroes of the Battle of Britain. He had contracted pneumonia earlier that winter and was still in a weakened condition when we had been marched out of Belaria. On this morning he staggered over to the side of the road, sat down beside the ditch, and announced that he'd "had it!" Several of his friends went over and remonstrated with him and tried to pull him to his feet.

"Let me alone!" he pleaded. "I've had it, I tell you . . . I'm not walking another bloody step!"

At this point the major walked up and, with his mud-caked boots spread apart and his peaked Luftwaffe cap pushed back on his head, stood looking down at the boy for several moments.

"My orders," he announced in his heavy accents, "are to shoot anyone who falls by the wayside."

Slowly he raised the flap on the holster of his Luger and, pulling out the weapon, stood with it pointing at the boy's forehead. The boy, sitting on the side of the ditch, looked up at him silently with all expression drained from his face, and for a minute or more the two remained in this silent tableau of death.

"What a hell of a way to die," I remember thinking to myself, "in a shit-filled ditch in Silesia . . ."

Then the major, still without saying anything, slowly returned the Luger to its holster and, walking over to the guards' supply wagon, pulled out a blanket.

"Here," he said, tossing it to the boy, "you'll need this. Tomorrow, maybe the Russians will find you . . ."

He spun on his heel then and, in an obvious effort to

cover up with military bombast what he considered a moment of weakness, began shouting at us. *"Marsch! Marsch!
Rechts raum! Marsch!"*

Later that day as we plodded along I found the major
walking beside me. *"Warum, Herr Major?"* I asked. "Why
did you not shoot that boy this morning?"

He was silent for a moment. "Ach . . . what would it
have proved?" Then stepping to the side of the road, he began bellowing at us, *"Rechts raum! Rechts raum!"*

By now our number had dwindled to an even one hundred: fifty men had either escaped and holed up to await
the Russians, had just fallen by the wayside, or had become
lost amidst the streaming horde of refugees. And then one
morning Brownie disappeared. For an hour Wally and I
had been treading along, sleepwalking, silently lost in our
own personal miseries, when we suddenly realized our friend
was not with us. As time passed we became increasingly worried about him, and both of us began to realize how important he had become to us. His unquenchable spirit, his
unflagging good humor, and the ability of his agile mind
to find something amusing or interesting in whatever befell
us had sustained us and kept us going through this march.
I especially would miss him, for of late I had fallen into
periodic and uncharacteristic moods of black depression.
There were times when I felt so battered and beaten by life
that I just wanted to crawl into a hole and lie there exhausted. My life appeared to be one long black joke per-
petrated by the gods, and this march was the culminating
piece of black humor. There had been times lately when I
too just wanted to sit down in the ditch and say, "The hell
with it!" But Brownie, more by example than any other
means, soon pulled me out of these moods of despair. A
truly estimable man was Kingsley Ewart Brown of Halifax,
Nova Scotia, and both Wally and I would miss him.

We were all but holding a requiem mass for this friend
of ours when suddenly he reappeared. The ever-present

twinkle was in his eyes, and the broad grin was intact, but this time he had about him the conspiratorial air of a cat who has just discovered a cache of cream. Falling in beside us, he silently opened up the verminous blanket he had taken to wearing about his shoulders like a shawl and showed us his discovered treasure. There nestling and bulging in the breast of his half-opened jacket were three loaves of German black bread! They might be rock crusted, stale, and sour, and they might contain quantities of sawdust, but they represented food, edible food, and they contained nourishment.

"Where in the hell did you . . . ?" Wally began, his hound-dog face lighting up with interest.

"Never mind"—Brownie laughed—"the Lord provides for those of us who are pure of heart. But, seriously . . . there's a group of Frenchmen back there—they've been slave laborers on farms in this area—and they've got a small cart with 'em loaded with bread. They must have a hundred loaves. I swapped my wrist watch for these three."

"Can you get any more?" Wally asked, taking off his watch.

"Sure . . . they're watch happy."

"But, good God," I started to protest, "a Rolex watch for three loaves of bread . . ."

"Goddamit, Harsh!" Wally shouted, agitated by the sight of all this food. "Give him your watch! You figured out a way to eat the bloody thing? You going to write a cookbook for the Rolex Watch Company? Let's get hold of all the bread we can get!"

"They promised for the next watch to throw in a bottle of *Schnaps*, too," Brownie added.

"That's different!" I grinned. "Why didn't you tell us that in the first place?"

"Jesus!" Wally snorted. "What a set of values!"

No one to this day has yet discovered what the Germans really intended to do with us, but by early March, 1945, they had moved us as far as the little town of Luckenwalde, thirty miles due south of Berlin. Outside this town was a large barbed-wire-enclosed compound, which the Germans were using as a catchall camp for the human flotsam and jetsam of a world turned upside-down, and it was into this camp they herded us. It was here the Russians finally overtook us.

The point of their advanced units reached us at seven o'clock one Sunday morning, and later the balance of the spearhead came. They came in jeeps, in armored cars, in weapons' carriers, trucks . . . they came on bicycles, on horseback, and on foot . . . and they came in huge, rumbling Stalin tanks. They came in wave after wave of fighters representing overwhelming fire power: there were Mongols and Tartars and White Russians and Ukrainians and Siberians and . . . They came in waves from all the far-flung components of the Union of Soviet Socialist Republics. And they were all drunk. The Russians were in a holiday mood, for at last they were in the heartland of a hated, stupidly heavy-handed conqueror. They were free to pillage and loot and rape and burn. Hitler's Third Reich had sown the dragon's teeth, and now it was reaping the full harvest.

After the spearhead had passed, the follow-up, occupying troops arrived, and they quickly separated us air force people from the civilians. They kept us for six weeks as they negotiated with the Americans on the west side of the Elbe River for an even exchange of liberated prisoners: we were to be exchanged for an equal number of Russian prisoners whom the Americans had liberated.

On the day of liberation we were driven to the Elbe in a convoy of Russian trucks. The Americans had thrown a pontoon bridge across the river, and now Dickie Collard, who was the senior officer among us, and the Russian *pahkawvnik*, or colonel, in charge of the operation, walked across the bridge to work out the final details of the transfer. In an hour Dickie and the colonel were back.

"All right, smartly now, chaps!" he shouted. "As soon as

three Russians cross the bridge three of you walk over."

Because I was the only American in the group my companions insisted that I cross over first. Brownie was right behind me, followed by Wally. As I got to the end of the bridge and just before I put my first step in three years on "free" soil, I was greeted by a big, rawboned American infantry colonel. He was standing at the end of the bridge, his hands on his hips, his helmet pushed back on his head, a big grin on his ugly weather-beaten face. I could have kissed him, he looked so beautiful.

"Here you are, chaps," he said with an exaggerated mock-British accent. "Right this way to Tokyo!"

For a moment I looked at him. "Fuck you, Jack," I said in pure gutter Americanese, "and the same goes for any friends you may have in . . . in California!"

It shook him. He had been expecting to greet one hundred well-bred, polite British officers. Instead he got me.

My choice of that fine, old, four-letter Saxon word meaning *to plant* was deliberate and carefully selected: it was exactly what I meant. Plant—bury—any so-called leaders of the human race who are too stupidly unimaginative to find a means other than war of settling the world's differences. And someday maybe the cannon fodder generation—those young people whom the leaders coerce into doing the actual fighting and killing and dying—will say to all such leaders exactly what I said to that American colonel. I not only have hope that this will come to pass—I have great faith.

Brownie, as though to emphasize his arrival, jumped down from the bridge with a hard-footed thump. "Well, what d'you know . . . ?" He grinned at me, slowly shaking his head.

Wally, with his doleful expression still in place, stepped down from the bridge with great dignity. Then turning to us, he said, "By God . . . we made it!"